Arranging & Describing

Archives & Manuscripts

A┃F┃S
ARCHIVAL
FUNDAMENTALS
SERIES II

Arranging & Describing

Archives & Manuscripts

KATHLEEN D. ROE

SOCIETY OF
American
Archivists

Chicago

The Society of American Archivists
www.archivists.org

©2005 by the Society of American Archivists.
All Rights Reserved.

Second printing 2006. Third printing 2008.

Library of Congress Cataloging-in-Publication Data
Roe, Kathleen, 1950-
  Arranging & describing archives & manuscripts / Kathleen D. Roe.
    p. cm. -- (Archival fundamentals series. II)
  Includes bibliographical references and index.
  ISBN 1-931666-13-X
  1. Archives. 2. Cataloging of manuscripts. I. Title: Arranging and describing
archives and manuscripts. II. Title. III. Series.

CD950.R64 2005
027--dc22
                                                        2005049036

Graphic design by Matt Dufek, dufekdesign@yahoo.com.
Fonts: Minion (text and footnotes); Meta (secondary text and captions).

TABLE *of* CONTENTS

Preface to the
ARCHIVAL FUNDAMENTALS SERIES II

There was a time when individuals entering the archival profession could read a few texts, peruse some journals, attend a workshop and institute or two, and walk away with a sense that they grasped the field's knowledge and discipline. This was an inadequate perception, of course, but it was true that the publications—basic or advanced, practical or theoretical—were modest in number.

The archival world has changed considerably since these more quiet times. A rich monographic research literature is developing. Scholars from far outside the field are examining the "archive" and the "record." Archives, archivists, records, and records managers are in the daily news as cases appear testing government and corporate accountability, organizational and societal memory, and the nature of documentary evidence—all challenging basic archival work and knowledge.

The new edition of the Archival Fundamentals Series (AFS II) is intended to provide the basic foundation for modern archival practice and theory. The original preface (written by Mary Jo Pugh in her capacity as the series editor) to the first editions, which were published in the early to mid-1990s by the Society of American Archivists (SAA), argued that the seven volumes "have been conceived and written to be a foundation for modern archival theory and practice" and aimed at "archivists, general practitioners and specialists alike, who are per- forming a wide range of archival duties in all types of archival and manuscript repositories." It is hard to state the purpose of the new AFS editions better.

There are some differences, both subtle and obvious, in the new volumes. The new editions are more open-ended than earlier versions, extending back to the Basic Manual Series published a quarter-of-a-century ago by SAA, reflecting evolving viewpoints about archival theory and practice. Even more important a difference is the broader and deeper context of archival publishing AFS volumes reside in. Mary Jo Pugh, in her introduction of just a decade ago, noted that the AFS titles are companions to "more specialized manuals also available from SAA." Now, SAA has four other series (some just underway), including Archival Classics (featuring reprints or new collections of older publications with pivotal importance to the profession), Archival Readers (both collections of new and previously published essays intended to supplement the descriptions of foundational theory and practice of the AFS II volumes), International Archival Studies Readers (both collections of new and previously published essays intended to provide glimpses of archival work and knowledge outside of North America), and Archival Cases and Case Studies (examining archival work in a variety of institutional types and with a variety of media). Added to SAA's own publications is a vast sea of new titles pouring from the presses of other professional associations and trade, professional, and university publishers.

Both the earlier Basic Manual Series and the Archival Fundamentals Series provide benchmarks in the development of archival knowledge and work. One can trace changing ideas and practices about archival reference services by reading the 1977, 1992, and 2004 volumes dedicated to this subject in the respective SAA manual series. One also expects to find in this volume current standards and consensus about this aspect of archival work. One also expects now, of course, that some may disagree with aspects of the current presentation, and may point to the growing research and case study literature being generated by the archival profession.

Many people participated in the production of the various volumes constituting the Archival Fundamentals Series II. The profession owes its gratitude not only to the authors, but to various chairs and members of the SAA Publications Board; Miriam Meislik, Photo

Editor for the series; the SAA Executive Directors, Susan Fox and Nancy P. Beaumont; and especially to Teresa Brinati, SAA Director of Publishing, whose good humor, organization, and steady commitment to a quality product helped keep the publishing of these and other SAA volumes on track.

RICHARD J. COX
Publications Editor
Society of American Archivists

Acknowledgments

As a description archivist, I cannot resist the opportunity to provide a "context" for this manual. The friends, colleagues, and family who have influenced, mentored, supported, and endured my work in archival description in general and this manual in particular deserve much more recognition and praise than either these acknowledgments or the limits of my language can provide.

I have had support and assistance from dedicated archival colleagues whose energy and talent have helped my understanding of archival description. Victoria Irons Walch has been an inspiration from the first Society of American Archivists meeting I attended. She has been a steadfast friend, always willing to share ideas about both archives and needlework with energy and an enviable sense of balance. In particular, she took on the onerous task of reviewing this manual not once but twice to ensure that it could be a publishable product. My deep appreciation also goes to Alden Monroe, my friend and frequent coconspirator, whose sheer good sense and incomparable laugh made it both energizing and just plain fun while we worked out the application of emerging descriptive standards with government records. Steven Hensen has been the "North Star" of description for me, always providing a steady brilliance and guidance in following the path of standardized practice. Teresa Brinati from SAA was enormously patient as I rewrote, rewrote, and rewrote this manual. Dennis Meissner provided welcome commentary and insight as the "mystery" reviewer for this manual.

Other colleagues shared their "in progress" work so I could improve the contents of this manual. Kris Kiesling graciously took time away from her own considerable responsibilities in coordinating the preparation of *Describing Archives: A Content Standard* to review and suggest ways we could integrate the wisdom of that important new archival tool into this manual. David Carmicheal shared his draft of the second edition of *Organizing Archival Records: A Practical Method of Arrangement and Description for Small Archives* along with his perceptive ideas on how to write clear and useful prose about description. With his unique panache and good cheer, Richard Pearce-Moses shared various versions of his *Glossary of Archives and Records Terminology*.

I also owe many debts "at home" to my current and former colleagues at the New York State Archives with whom I've shared a wild range of descriptive experiences as we've tried to provide access to the behemoth that is New York's history and government. And I cannot let the opportunity go by to acknowledge Professor Philip P. Mason from Wayne State University, and Geneva Kebler Wiskemann from the Michigan State Archives who shared their incomparable passion for archives with me in a way so compelling I changed careers to join this profession.

My daughter Kate with her many passions and enthusiasms in life provided a unique source of inspiration for this manual. I am also deeply indebted to my husband, James Corsaro, himself a manuscripts curator, who listened, encouraged, and often simply endured the writing of this manual. They are among the few things in life I find totally beyond the power of description.

Introduction

Archival records are identified and maintained because they have permanent value for an incalculable number and range of users. Arrangement and description are essential to ensure that the records so carefully and conscientiously brought into the archives are indeed comprehensible and accessible for reference purposes. Despite this pivotal role, for much of the twentieth century archival practices of arrangement and description in individual institutions might most charitably be called eclectic. Fortunately, since SAA published its first manual on arrangement and description in 1977,[1] significant developments in the standardization of this function have taken place in the United States, Canada, and internationally. This manual is intended to provide an overview of the fundamental theory and practice relating to archival arrangement and description, drawing particularly on the substantive codification and standardization of practice over the past quarter of a century.

Specifically, the goals for this manual are

- to provide a context for understanding the purpose and goals of archival arrangement and description;

---

1 In 1977, SAA published David B. Gracy II's *Archives and Manuscripts: Arrangement and Description,* and in 1990 Frederic M. Miller's *Arranging and Describing Archives and Manuscripts,* which this manual replaces, as part of SAA's Archival Fundamentals Series.

- to provide an introduction to the core principles that are the foundation of archival arrangement and description;
- to define core terminology relating to arrangement and description;
- to introduce the common practices and professional standards used in arranging and describing archives and manuscripts; and
- to provide information on current and emerging developments and approaches in archival arrangement and description.

A wide range of individuals need basic information on arrangement and description of archival records. This manual aims to provide the necessary theoretical and practical framework regarding archival arrangement and description for individuals with archival responsibilities who want to make their materials accessible in a standardized manner that allows for integration with national/international access tools, but follows accepted practices. This may include those who are in the initial stages of formal archival education and individuals who are learning archival practice "on the job," as well as librarians, museum curators, and records managers who have responsibilities for archival or manuscript materials as part of other duties.

This manual consists of four sections:

1. The overview for this manual places arrangement and description within the context of archival functions. It also addresses the relationship of arrangement and description to archival repositories and users.

2. The section on core concepts and principles for arrangement and description defines the essential terminology and principles serving as the foundation for this function. It also compares and contrasts archival descriptive practice to comparable functions in the library and museum professions. Finally, it considers the relationship of descriptive practice to the individual institutional mission.

3. The context of arrangement and description provides summary background on the development of archival descriptive practices primarily in the United States, but also including Canadian and international developments. Since many fine works address

earlier developments, focus here is on more recent developments particularly as they relate to automated access.

4. The practice of arrangement and description provides an overview of the steps in arranging and describing archival records. It provides information on common elements of information collected at various stages, types of access tools, and current standards.

Illustrations and examples support the principles and practices being described in this manual. Three hypothetical core examples are provided and expanded at various points to demonstrate processes being explained. Illustrations based on examples from actual repositories appear throughout the manual and in the appendices, but the reader should be advised that these might have been truncated or modestly adapted for purposes of illustrating a point in the text of the manual. They should not necessarily be considered "models" for completed descriptive tools. An effort also was made to include examples of the wide range of materials found in archives, as well as of regional and cultural diversity.

A glossary provides definitions of the terms found in italics throughout the manual.

The appendices provide a bibliography of books, articles, and Web sites of potential interest, as well as examples too extensive to be incorporated in the manual text.

This manual addresses many changes that have occurred in descriptive practice in the decade since Miller's *Arranging and Describing Archives and Manuscripts* was published. Nonetheless, arrangement and description continue to be subject to additional changes and developments, particularly in the area of professional standards and rules in this area, and in the types of access tools made possible through automated approaches. Within a short time of its publication, readers of this manual will need to refer to contemporary archival literature for the most current status of practice in those areas.

Chapter 1

Overview

The Nature of Archives and Manuscripts

Substantial professional debate has been invested in drawing the distinctions between archives and manuscripts, but their similarities predominate for the purposes of arrangement and description. In this manual, commonly accepted definitions are drawn from several sources including *A Glossary of Archival and Records Terminology* or its predecessor edition,[2] *Describing Archives: A Content Standard (DACS),*[3] and the International Council on Archives' *ISAD(G): General International Standard Archival Description.*[4] The term *archives* technically refers to the permanently valuable records received and accumulated by formal organizations such as governments, businesses, and nonprofit organizations in the process of conducting their daily business. The term *manuscripts* commonly refers to valuable historical or literary records of people or families created, received, assembled, or accumulated as they conducted their daily personal activities.

---

2 Richard Pearce-Moses, comp., *A Glossary of Archival and Records Terminology* (Chicago: Society of American Archivists, 2005); Lewis J. Bellardo and Lynn Lady Bellardo, comps., *A Glossary for Archivists, Manuscripts Curators, and Records Managers* (Chicago: Society of American Archivists, 1992).

3 Society of American Archivists, *Describing Archives: A Content Standard* (Chicago: Society of American Archivists, 2004).

4 International Council on Archives, *ISAD(G): General International Standard Archival Description,* 2nd ed. (Ottawa: ICA, 2000).

Figure 1-1 Examples of Archives and Manuscripts

***Archives* are the permanently valuable records of organizations, businesses, and government.**	*Archives:* • Burden Iron Company. Record of employees dismissed. • Brandywine Trout and Conservation Club. Minutes of the Board of Directors. • Michigan State University. History Department. Course evaluations. • Davis County (Utah). County Auditor. Tax exempt properties records.
***Manuscripts* are the historical or literary records of people and families.**	*Manuscripts:* • Virginia Foster Durr Papers. • Justo Martí Photograph Collection. • Thomas Cole Sketchbooks. • Aisenshtin Family Oral History Interviews.

To complicate this terminology, in common parlance the term *archives* frequently encompasses both the records of organizations and people, as well as referring to the actual type of organization that retains permanently valuable records. In the course of this manual, the term *archives* will be used in the broader sense, referring to permanently valuable records, whether maintained by individuals or organizations. Examples will be provided throughout representing both organizational and personal records.

Of perhaps more importance to defining archives and manuscripts are the phrases "permanently valuable" and "created, accumulated, assembled, or maintained in the conduct of daily activities." The designation of permanent value indicates a reason to keep the records in perpetuity for current and/or future use. The need to ensure users have the ability to identify and locate records over decades and even centuries poses awesome challenges for archivists. Similarly, archival records are unique in that they are byproducts of human activity. The reason for or method by which they were "created, accumulated, assembled, or maintained in the conduct of daily activities" has important influence on the arrangement and description that follow. In this organic nature of archives and manuscripts the archivist confronts another significant range of challenges. The importance of the context in which records were created, their roles or functions, and the uses made of them by the "records creator" are essential elements affecting the practice of arrangement and description.

Archives are not simply "old" paper of some indeterminate age and level of dustiness, rescued from an old closet, attic, or flea market. Archivists are increasingly managing permanently valuable records from the time of their creation or working with records managers and records creators to do so. This approach can be important for paper records, but it is even more so for electronic records and nonpaper records. Increasingly archivists recognize that good records management, whether personal or organizational, is important to ensure the integrity of the records.

Archives and manuscripts also include a range of format types beyond traditional paper, including moving images, audiotapes, photographs, maps and geographic information systems, and electronic record systems. The concepts underlying the principles and practices of arrangement and description remain the same regardless of physical format, although some additions and adjustments may be necessary.

Archival principles for arrangement and description apply to all forms of material.

Archival principles for arrangement and description also apply to intentionally assembled collections of archives and manuscripts. For a wide variety of reasons, individuals or organizations may collect historical records relating to a topic, person, event, or period. The resulting collections have permanent value both in their informational content and the context in which they were created.

Archival Repositories and Their Clientele

Who holds archival records? A 1998 survey done by the Council of State Historical Records Coordinators and reported in *Where History Begins*

Figure 1-2 Types of Archives and Manuscripts Repositories

Types	Examples
Historical societies/ archival repositories	
• Regional historical societies	Millet and District Historical Society San Diego Historical Society
• Special topic archives	New Orleans Jazz and Heritage Foundation Archives Railroad Museum of Pennsylvania
Academic institutions	
• College/university	Texas Southern University Archives University of British Columbia Archives
• Elementary/second-ary school	Phillips Exeter Academy Archives Punahou School Archives
Public libraries	Ft. Wayne Public Library Coeur d'Alene Public Library
Museums	Woods Hole Historical Museum Archives Boston Museum of Fine Arts Archives
Records creators • Businesses	Digital Equipment Corporation Corporate Archives NBC News Archives
• Religious organizations	Archdiocese of Cincinnati Archives Moravian Archives

(continued)

Figure 1-2 continued

Types	Examples
• Nonprofit organizations	National Ballet of Canada Archives Hispanic Society of America
• Medical institutions	Columbia-Presbyterian Medical Center Archives Maine Medical Center Library Hospital Archives
• Native American tribes	Mashantucket Pequot Museum and Research Center Akwesasne Library and Cultural Center
• Unions	Foundation of the New York State Nurses Association Archives Walter P. Reuther Library Archives of Labor and Urban Affairs
Governments • National	u.s. National Archives and Records Administration National Archives of Canada
• State/provincial/ territorial	North Dakota State Archives Archives of Ontario
• County/city/regional	Dallas Municipal Archives and Research Center Troup County (GA) Archives

indicates a significant number of organizations manage archives and manuscripts in the United States.[5] Some of those have the administration of an archival collection as their primary mission, others combine that administration with management of other cultural resources (such as a museum or library), and yet others manage archives as part of a larger business, social, or professional organization.

The mission of the parent organization and the manner in which the archives supports that mission will affect the type of records deemed permanently valuable. It will also influence aspects of arrangement and description and the types of users for whom the archival records are being made accessible. For example, in corporate archives, the primary users will be the corporation's staff. Most likely, the archivist will conduct a considerable amount of the searching for relevant records and often will need to facilitate quick, specific item access for corporate users. This places substantially different demands on the arrangement and description process than one would find in archives whose primary clientele are historians seeking every possible record created by or relating to their subject of research and who will want to review the access tools and records themselves. Different still is the historical society where genealogists seek name access. While the varying nature of the institutional mission and clientele will affect the arrangement and description process, the essential principles and practices can still be applied, with adjustments in level or intensity of detail to meet the particular situation.

The Function of Arrangement and Description

As succinctly stated in the ISAD(G) *General International Standard Archival Description,* Second Edition, "the purpose of archival description is to identify and explain the context and content of archival material in order to promote its accessibility."[6] To accomplish that purpose, the archivist must first arrange records, that is, identify the intellectual

---

5   Victoria Irons Walch, comp., *Where History Begins: A Report on Historical Records Repositories in the United States* (Council of State Historical Records Coordinators, May 1998) available on-line at http://www.coshrc.org/reports/HRRS/hrrsdocs.html.

6   International Council, ISAD(G), 7.

pattern existing in the materials, then make sure their physical organization reflects that pattern. Following arrangement and drawing from it, the archivist describes the records. This involves developing a summary "representation" or access tool that includes information on the context in which the materials were created, their physical characteristics, and their informational content. The descriptive information can be provided through a range of finding aids and access tools to help users to assess records for their relevance to a research need. Essentially, *arrangement* addresses the physical organization of records while *description* is the process used to provide information about the context and content of records.

The purpose of arrangement and description is to promote access.

Students from East Aurora High School consulting records for a class research project. The range of researchers seeking access to archival records poses challenges for arrangement and description. PHOTOGRAPH COURTESY NEW YORK STATE ARCHIVES.

The Relationship of Arrangement and Description to Other Archival Functions

The poet Marianne Moore wrote that "it's all connected," an observation that is certainly true about the relationship of arrangement and description to the other primary archival functions. Arrangement and description build on the work in the functions preceding it and provide the infrastructure upon which other archival functions build.

> RECORDS MANAGEMENT. Records with archival value need to be identified early in their *life cycle*. Organizations with competent records-management programs ensure records are managed in a way that supports the identification of permanently valuable groups of records and that necessary information about the creation and use of the records survives for use by the archives. The importance of records management to arrangement and description is especially significant with electronic records, where key system documentation must be saved to preserve the records and make them accessible. The records of individuals pose greater records-management challenges as the value of personal papers may not be recognized until a career or life is well along, if not over. Additionally, with only a few exceptions, individuals rarely produce enough records to warrant a "records manager." Nonetheless, donating individuals and families can provide important insight on the manner in which records were kept, and the uses to which they were put, which are essential for arrangement and description.

> APPRAISAL AND ACQUISITION. Essential information for arrangement and description can be identified at the point of appraisal and acquisition. During appraisal, contextual information is identified that helps explain why the records are important. Conversely, arrangement and description can affect appraisal and acquisition as well. However good and focused the appraisal or collecting policy may be, poor quality or obscure description can render the records "unfindable."

> PRESERVATION. Basic preservation is intimately entwined with arrangement and description, since foldering, reboxing, and iden-

tifying preservation problems often happen during accessioning and description. While undertaking arrangement and description, the archivist or technical staff often uncovers particular preservation problems or needs.

REFERENCE. Arrangement and description are perhaps most intimately connected with reference services because the purpose of description is to make the records accessible for users. The finding aids produced as part of description are essential tools to help users, whether on- or off-site, to identify relevant materials. With the introduction of the Internet and on-line catalogs, the reference process depends even more on the type and quality of descriptive products developed, as users may never talk directly with an archivist.

Users also influence the arrangement and description of records. Search strategies commonly employed, predominant types of users, and the level of support provided by the reference staff to users should all have a profound affect on the type and level of arrangement and description, as well as the types of access tools developed by descriptive staff. The archival profession has begun to assess the information-seeking behaviors of users, and some analysis has been done of how users perceive archival access tools, but much work remains in this area.[7]

PUBLIC PROGRAMMING AND OUTREACH. As with reference services, types of public programs and outreach initiatives will both depend on and affect arrangement and description. For example, a museum with an archival collection may rely on the archival photographic holdings to support its exhibit program. In such a case, access to photographic holdings may be made available at a more detailed level, and staff members may identify "exhibit qual-

7   See, for example, Paul Conway, "Research in Presidential Libraries: A User Study," *Midwestern Archivist* 11, no. 1 (1986): 35–56; Barbara Craig, "Old Myths in New Clothes: Expectation of Archives Users," *Archivaria* 45 (1998): 118–26; Wendy Duff and Penka Stoyanova, "Transforming the Crazy Quilt: Archival Displays from a User's Point of View," *Archivaria* 45 (1998): 44–79; James M. Roth, "Serving Up EAD: An Exploratory Study on the Deployment and Utilization of Encoded Archival Description Finding Aids," *American Archivist* 64, no. 2 (2001): 214–37.

ity" items for future use as descriptive work is underway. For an organization such as a regional historical society working with local teachers, the descriptive access tools and finding aids may be developed using terminology and identifying prime collections for that specific audience. Other archives with substantial birth, death, and marriage records may choose to develop special name indexes and tools for their genealogical patrons.

Educational outreach efforts help users of archives learn more about the archives and its collections and may even enhance the researcher's skills in working with archival materials. PHOTOGRAPH COURTESY ALMA FISHER, TOUGALOO COLLEGE.

Chapter 2

Core Concepts and Principles of Arrangement and Description

Defining Basic Terms

Arrangement and description are the essential processes by which an archivist gains intellectual and physical control over a body of records. They are intertwined, interdependent functions with arrangement providing the framework for description, while information obtained to describe records provides insight on the arrangement pattern. Arrangement involves identifying the intellectual structure of records, then physically organizing those records following the accepted archival principles of provenance and original order.

> Definition: Arrangement is the process of organizing materials with respect to their provenance and original order, to protect their context, and to achieve physical and intellectual control over the materials.

Where a structure either does not exist or was disturbed, the archivist should establish an order relying on the principles of *provenance* and *original order* insofar as possible. Both the concept and practices of physical arrangement are most applicable in a paper-

Figure 2-1 *Describing Archives: A Content Standard (DACS)*

Following is an abbreviated version of the statement of principles codified in *DACS*. The full statement is contained in appendix A.

Statement of Principles

The Nature of Archival Holdings
Archival collections are the natural result of the activities of individuals and organizations and serve as the recorded memory thereof. This distinctive relationship between records and the activities that generated them differentiates archives from other documentary resources.

Principle 1: Records in archives possess unique characteristics.

Principle 2: The principle of *respect des fonds* is the basis of archival arrangement and description.

The Relationship between Arrangement and Description
Arrangement is the intellectual and/or physical processes of organizing documents in accordance with accepted archival principles as well as the results of these processes. Description is the creation of an accurate representation of the archival material by the process of capturing, collating, analyzing, and organizing information that serves to identify archival material and to explain the context and records systems that produced it.

Principle 3: Arrangement involves the identification of groupings within the material.

Principle 4: Description reflects arrangement.

The Nature of Archival Description
Archival holdings are varied in their nature and provenance. Archival description reflects that. If they are to be described consistently within an institutional, regional, or national descriptive system, the rules must apply to a variety of forms and media created by, and acquired from, a variety of sources.

(continued)

Figure 2-1 continued

Principle 5: Description applies to all archival materials regardless of form or medium.

Principle 6: The principles of archival description apply equally to records created by corporate bodies and by individuals or families.

Principle 7: Archival descriptions may be presented in a variety of outputs and with varying levels of detail.

Principle 7.1: Levels of description correspond to the levels of arrangement.

Principle 7.2: Relationships between levels of description must be clearly indicated.

Principle 7.3: Information provided at each level of description must be appropriate to that level.

The Creators of Archival Material
An important aspect of understanding archival materials is the description of the context in which they were created.

Principle 8: The creators of archival materials, as well as the materials themselves, must be described.

based environment. Clearly, the practices used for paper records are not directly translatable to electronic records in such areas as "physical arrangement." Conceptually, however, electronic records often are organized in records systems that are useful in expressing provenance-based conceptual relationships revealing how records were used by an organization or person.

Definition: Description is the creation of an accurate representation of a unit of archival material by the process of capturing, collating, analyzing, and organizing information that serves to identify archival material and explain the context and records system(s) that produced it.

Traditionally, archivists tend to equate the definition of description with providing access to holdings through the development of finding aids. It is, however, much more than the products that may result. Description is an organic process—it may, and perhaps preferably should, begin early in the life cycle of a record series or group of manuscripts. It also may continue after a formal "finding aid" is initially written. Insights provided by users may lead to the addition of information or indexing terms to the original descriptive product, or further material (an accrual or accretion) may be added to the group of records, resulting in changes to the finding aid. New historical insights, information, or cultural understandings may also result in further description or revision.

Archival description, unlike library cataloging, also goes beyond the content and physical description of the records themselves. Information to manage and interpret the records is also essential to description. For example, it may be important for the archivist to know what preservation treatments were used over time so that conflicting chemicals or approaches will not be used. Similarly, understanding the context in which records were created, by whom, the era during which records were created, or the purpose for which the records were used may affect how a user interprets the content of those records.

Archivists in both the United States and Canada have developed specific standards for the arrangement and description of archives and manuscripts. These tools provide detailed rules and recommended practices beyond the scope of this manual. Archivists in the U.S. should refer to *Describing Archives: A Content Standard (DACS)* for further guidance. In Canada, *Rules for Archival Description,* Second Edition (*RAD2*) provides the rules and practices.

Core Principles Guiding the Practice of Arrangement and Description

The principles of provenance and original order are the foundations of archival arrangement and description. These principles direct the archivist to respect the integrity of the manner in which records were originally created, accumulated, assembled, and used rather than imposing some artificial order based on possible uses or classification schemes. This approach reflects the essential assumption that records have two levels of information users need to understand. Records have *content,* thereby providing specific factual data as well as attitudes and views from a particular person's or organization's perspective. Records also reflect the *context* in which they were created. For example, the congressional records of Barbara Jordan contain factual information on her Watergate Committee service and her interactions with constituents, as well as her opinions on a range of political and social issues. The context in which they were created is also important because they provide insight into the experiences of an African American woman in the u.s. Congress in the 1970s.

Content is the actual information in records—what subjects and issues are addressed in the records.

Context is the conditions under or during which records were created—a historical era, a social milieu.

Provenance is defined as "the relationship between records and the organizations or individuals that created, accumulated, and/or maintained and used them in the conduct of personal or corporate activity."[9] The principle of provenance states that records should be maintained according to their origin and not "intermingled" with those of another provenance, that is those created by another person or agency. They should be kept

The principle of provenance states that records should be maintained according to their origin and not "intermingled" with those of another provenance, that is those created by another person or agency.

together on the basis of the organization or person that created, used, or accumulated the group of records and in the groupings of records the person or organization created. Provenance is crucial because it reveals important information about the *context* in which records were created. That context influences the content and coverage of records and can provide information on the attitudes reflected by the records.

The principle of original order involves keeping records in the order in which they were kept by the person or organization that created, accumulated, assembled, or maintained them. The groupings, file system,

---

9   Society of American Archivists, *Describing Archives: A Content Standard.*

Figure 2-2 The Effect of Context on Records

The context of creation affects the content and "attitude" of these records relating to the Love Canal and the issue of toxic waste dumps. Each of the organizations or individuals creating the records had a particular function, activity, or purpose for their work that affects the content or perspectives in the records.

Hooker Chemical and Plastics Corp. Records: Business records relating to the company's manufacturing and supplying of organic and inorganic chemicals, additives and intermediates, technology and equipment to industries throughout the world.

Ecumenical Task Force (ETF) of the Niagara Frontier, Inc., Records: Records of the ETF, which provided direct aid to Love Canal residents, provided an advocacy voice for the religious community on behalf of the residents, and worked toward long-range solutions to the chemical waste problems locally and throughout the country.

Adeline Levine Papers: Reports, documents, photocopies of correspondence, and other material used by Dr. Adeline Levine, Department of Sociology at the State University of New York at Buffalo, as background for her book, *Love Canal: Science, Politics and People.*

New York State Legislature Assembly Task Force on Toxic Substances: Reports and hearing files from the task force's investigation of toxic waste dumping at the Love Canal and its impact on the surrounding community.

The principle of original order states that records should be maintained in the order established by the person or organization that created, accumulated, assembled, or maintained them. subdivisions, and other physical structuring provided by the records creator should be maintained. Keeping records in the order the creator kept them provides information about the context and use of those records. This can be critical information if the archivist is to accurately represent information about manuscripts or archival records. It can also have substantive significance for the user in analyzing and interpreting records.

Archival arrangement and description apply to all forms of material found in a group of records. Whether that group consists of one single form, from paper to photographs, architectural drawings to electronic media, or if those media are mixed together in a group of records, they are still maintained together for arrangement and description. To do otherwise would destroy the provenance and original order of the records and compromise the accurate representation of the context and content.[10]

What "Entity" Should Be Described?

Following the principles of provenance and original order, archives and manuscripts are most commonly and most appropriately described at an aggregate or collective level. That is, they are described in the same groupings that were created by the person or organization responsible for the records.

Organizations and individuals create groups of records as part of their daily life or business. Those groups are created, collected, used, or maintained together to fulfill a particular function, activity, or role for the person or organization. The records need to be arranged and described in a manner that supports a user's understanding of how the records were created and originally used. Archivists sometimes refer to the "first level of description," meaning the most general grouping in which records were created and used for a function, activity, or role. All records should be arranged and described beginning with that first level of description. With complex groups of records, or those with extremely rich content for users, more detailed levels of description may be appropriate.

In collective description, related items are described as a unified whole.[11]

Within these groupings, records may be described at different levels of detail in different situations. Some records, particularly those created in the latter half of the twentieth century and after, can consist of complex records systems with several parts and subparts. For other

---

10 For purposes of physical preservation, certain types of records may be stored separately, but they are included in the intellectual arrangement and description.

11 Pearce-Moses, *Archival and Records Terminology.*

Figure 2-3 Sample Records

These three groups of records were created for the purposes of illustration. They will be used throughout this manual to demonstrate practices being discussed. Complete descriptions for each are contained in appendix D.

Charles E. Williams, a prominent African American lawyer in New York City, has died. His family finds in his home office a file cabinet with two drawers, one marked "personal" containing letters, the other marked "school" containing various papers relating to his elementary and high school years. In his office at the law firm of Peck, Williams, and Wilson they find files from the various legal cases he worked on.

The materials in the home office are *personal papers* that reflect various aspects of Williams's youth and personal life. They should be treated as a separate entity for description. The files in his office reflect his professional work as a lawyer and are in fact records of the law firm and its functions. As such they would be addressed as part of the records-management program of the law firm, not as Williams's own papers.

Annie Maxwell, the town clerk of Hot Coffee, Nevada, has received a grant to inventory her records and describe those that are archival. In the town clerk's office are file cabinets with the following: town board meeting minutes; planning board meeting minutes; hunting and fishing licenses; and election records. These are not personal papers of Annie Maxwell, as they were created to fulfill her function as the town clerk and include records from the previous six town clerks as well. Each of the groups reflects a different function of the town clerk's office and should be described as individual entities within the group of records created by the town clerk.

Katherine Valdez, a physical education professor at Asuncion College, has collected letters, videotapes, posters, and other materials relating to synchronized swimming and in particular to Esther Williams. On her retirement, she donates these materials to the local historical society. The materials do not result from her professional work as a physical education instructor nor was the collecting of such materials part of her duties as a faculty member. They will be described as an assembled collection because they were collected by Professor Valdez as part of her avocational interest in synchronized swimming.

records, the informational content and the need of users for access to it may necessitate more detailed description. The arrangement structure of a manuscript group or archival records will serve as a useful tool in determining what should be described.

Differences between Canadian and international descriptive practices and those in the United States relate to how the initial level of description is determined. Both identify an essential first level of description.

Canadian and international practice identify the first level as the fonds for both archival and manuscripts materials. The *fonds* is defined as "the whole of the documents, regardless of form or medium, automatically and organically created and/or accumulated and used by a particular individual, family or corporate body in the course of that creator's activities or functions."[12]

In the United States, records-keeping traditions have resulted in records being aggregated in a variety of ways so one all-encompassing concept like *fonds* is not necessarily applicable. The long and complex debate over the concepts of *fonds,* manuscript group, assembled collection, record group, and series as the first level for description is beyond the realm of this manual to settle. Differences in records creation and recordkeeping traditions in the United States at the organizational and personal levels necessitate the flexibility reflected in practice relating to the entity to be described. Nonetheless, arrangement and description must accurately reflect the way records were created and used by the person or organization by careful application of the principles of provenance and original order.

Figure 2-4 Examples of Fonds

- Canadian Labour Congress fonds, 1849–1992
- Eva Langbord fonds, 1926–1992
- Order Sons of Italy of Canada fonds, 1915–1990
- Fonds Association des scouts du Canada, 1914–1985

---

12 International Council, ISAD(G), 10.

As practice has developed in the u.s., the first level of description is determined based on a careful assessment of the context in which the records were created and the nature of the records being described. While following the principles of provenance and original order in determining the group or "entity" to be described, there are some differences in terminology and approach for records created by individuals and families, those created by organizations, and those consisting of assembled collections. An explanation of the approaches used for each follows.

Many of the valuable records in historical societies, libraries, and other archival collections reflect the lives and activities of individuals. The terms *manuscript group* or *collection* are generally used to represent the organic collectivity of records created, accumulated, assembled, or used by a person or family.[13] Because of the varied nature of records kept by individuals or families, these records are often described at the manuscript group level. Again, in some cases, the complexity or extent of these records may lead to more detailed arrangement and description.

With personal papers, the archivist often faces a complicated situation when determining the entity to describe. Much will depend on the manner in which the individual maintained his or her records and the quantity of records involved. For the most part, personal papers are described as an aggregate based on the individual or family. Since individuals are intimately involved in their own lives, they can manage their personal papers with a considerable degree of disorder. As a result, when papers from a person or family are donated to a manuscript library or archives, the original order of the records may not be entirely clear, and in some cases, it is not possible to determine just who created or accumulated a group of records. With the exception of more modern personal papers, the extent of those records is often small enough to describe entirely at the most aggregate level. (See figure 2-5.)

Organizations are a major source of archival records, particularly in the modern era. In the process of doing their business they almost automatically create records. Records created by organizations generally reflect their specific functions or activities regardless of whether they are

---

13 The term *collection* is used in a variety of ways in the u.s., which can lead to some confusion between records created by one individual or organization and intentionally assembled collections. In this manual, the term *collection* is used exclusively to refer to intentionally assembled collections.

Figure 2-5 Levels of Description for Personal
and Family Papers

Personal and family papers are often described at the broader level.
These examples provide title level only, not the full descriptive notes:

Records described at the manuscript group level only.	• Gertrude Wolf Papers, 1899–1942 • Ximenes Family Papers, 1828–1842

In some cases, sufficient complexity exists to necessitate a more detailed
description:

Records described at the manuscript group level and then at the series level.	Pura Belpré Papers, 1896–1985 • Personal and Biographical Information, 1919–1985 • Correspondence, 1921–1982 • Writings, 1932–1980 • Subject Files, 1896–1982 • Photographs, 1900–1980

a nonprofit organization, a business, a government, or a social organization. In some cases, the archival records of organizations are described as a record group. In the United States, the National Archives and some state archives and organizations or corporations describe records at this level of

> A record group is all the records produced by a government agency or an organization in the process of doing its business.

aggregation, then, as useful, describe records at the series level. Other organizational and governmental archives, however, use the series level as the first level of aggregation for description, as does the Australian government.[14] This practice has developed because the actual creation of files

14 For more on the government records issues relating to this, see Peter Scott, "The Record Group Concept: A Case for Abandonment," *American Archivist* 29 (October 1966): 493–504; Max Evans, "Authority Control: An Alternative to the Record Group Concept," *American Archivist* 49 (April 1986): 249–61; and Bob Krawczyk, "Cross Reference Heaven: The Abandonment of the Fonds as the Primary Level of Arrangement for Ontario Government Records," *Archivaria* 48 (Fall 1999): 131–53.

Personal papers often consist of multiple formats and lack precise order. Photograph courtesy Town of Bovina (NY) Historian.

occurs at lower levels in the organizational hierarchy and reflects specific functions. Records systems in these organizations are not designed to coordinate from the agency level and do not have an intrinsic relationship. In addition, description at the series level accommodates organizational changes and restructuring that may cause a change in who administers a function and a group of records, but results in no other changes to the series.

Determining what entity to describe for organizational records is generally less complicated because both private and governmental organizations tend to create and manage records in defined filing systems due to the volume, the number of users, and the need for accountability. An organization's records may also cover a significant period of time, with many individuals involved in creating and using them. In the United States, organizational records are generally described based on the series created by that organization. A series is a "file unit or documents arranged in accordance with a

> In the u.s., organizational records are usually described based on the series. A series is a group of records created or maintained in a unit because they result from the same activity or function.

filing system or maintained as a unit because they result from the same accumulation or filing process, the same function, or the same activity; have a particular form; or because of some other relationship arising out of their creation, receipt, or use."[15] In some cases, so few records survive from an organization that a single description of all the records will suffice. However, for most organizations, particularly those from the modern era, the volume and complexity of records makes description at the series level most useful.

Figure 2-6 Levels of Description for Organizational Records

Some archivists describe records first at the records group level, then at the series level. Others create an administrative history and only describe records at the series level.

See appendix E for record group description (example 10) and for an administrative history and series description (example 17).

Series created and maintained by Kentucky State University, Office of the President, each of which has been described at the series level, include

- Correspondence files, 1950–1988
- Budgets, 1931–1970
- Faculty minutes, 1896–1969
- Administrative council minutes, 1976–1979
- Southern Association of Colleges and Schools accreditation files, 1940–1970
- Capital construction files, 1958–1976
- Special event program files, 1913–1966

In cases where limited records exist and series-level description is not necessary, organizational records can be described at a larger aggregation:

- Texas Land and Live Stock Company (Austin, Tex.) records, 1906–1929 (1 document box)
- Christ Church (Durham Parish, Md.) records, 1774–1927 (1 cubic ft.)

Repositories with manuscripts and personal paper holdings also may have intentionally assembled collections of historical records. Generally, these collections result from an individual or group literally "collecting" papers, letters, photographs, or other archival records

---

15 Bellardo and Bellardo, *A Glossary for Archivists, Manuscripts Curators, and Records Managers,* 32.

based on a theme or interest area. During the nineteenth century, a number of important manuscript collectors, such as Peter Force, sought to document the colonial and early statehood period in the United States by avidly seeking out and amassing significant collections of manuscripts. In other cases, a group or organization may find that records have been so dispersed that they have to find and "reassemble" records for their community. Like records created by individuals and organizations in the process of doing their daily business, these collections have a context of creation that necessitates their being described using archival practices.

Figure 2-7 Examples of Assembled Collections

- Effa Manley collection of Negro League baseball cards
- Percy B. Lovell cartoon collection
- Food marketing collection
- Charlotte Hanes Harding autographs collection
- Far Rockaway (N.Y.) local history collection
- Sokagon Chippewa Community tribal archives project collection

Both organizational records and personal papers can also be subdivided into series or subseries, as indicated in the examples, and described at these increasing levels of specificity when it makes them more comprehensible and accessible. Records should, however, first be described at the broader aggregate level, then, if useful, additional description should be provided for the more specific level. Records should never be described at the most specific levels without a broader level of description. In the past, some archives and manuscript libraries described records at the item level without arranging and describing those records at the higher levels of series or manuscripts group. While well intentioned, that approach robs the user of the ability to see the context or provenance of the records and could lead to serious misinterpretations. Item-level description is now considered by archivists to be

Item level description should never occur without broader level description being provided.

appropriate only on rare occasions for records of extreme importance. In some cases, item-level description might be done for a few critical items within the series or manuscript group, but it should always be presented within the context of the broader group of records.

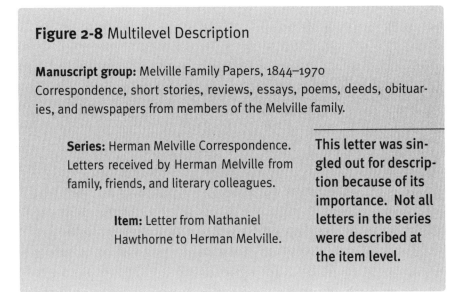

Figure 2-8 Multilevel Description

Manuscript group: Melville Family Papers, 1844–1970
Correspondence, short stories, reviews, essays, poems, deeds, obituaries, and newspapers from members of the Melville family.

Series: Herman Melville Correspondence. Letters received by Herman Melville from family, friends, and literary colleagues.

Item: Letter from Nathaniel Hawthorne to Herman Melville.

This letter was singled out for description because of its importance. Not all letters in the series were described at the item level.

The Relationship of Archival Descriptive Practice to Libraries and Museums

A significant number of historical societies, archives, libraries, and museums hold a mixture of archival records, library materials, and artifacts. Individuals in smaller organizations must often single-handedly manage access to these different types of materials. In defining its own conceptual base for arrangement and description more clearly, the archival profession has had to better define archival practice, and also differentiate it from the practices of these other two professional disciplines. Those distinctions can help the archivist determine which professional methodologies are most appropriate for portions of the overall historical collection.

The most obvious difference is the physical characteristics. Books have a standardized structure resulting from a long history and tradition of publishing. A book will generally have a title page, table of contents, chapters, indexes, and so forth. Even the physical format and size of books are fairly standardized and similar across nations, especially those in Latin-based languages. Archival materials lack a standardized structure beyond such a basic level as the paper sizes agreed on for business purposes, and even those are limited. More commonly, archival records, such as diaries, field books, and bound volumes, vary considerably in size. Archival maps can range from small items to huge rolled maps to those in a GIS system. Electronic records particularly push the boundaries with the many software and hardware issues that enter into the descriptive process. Museum materials vary most of all in size, format, and physical composition, as they are primarily nontextual. They can include a 1920s automobile, a sixth-century chalice, and a twentieth-century photograph. Confusion most obviously arises with items such as photographs, maps, and oral histories.

A second defining characteristic separating library, archives, and museum materials is the purpose for which they were created. In general, books are created to stand alone, to be read from beginning to end, and to focus on a topic, theme, person, and so forth. Each book can be used independently of the other books in the library. Archival materials, whether personal, organizational, or group, are created in the process of "doing" business or life activities. They are the vehicle for carrying information about the functions or roles of people, groups or organizations, and they do not have a predefined focus. Museum materials are also not "autonomous" in the way library materials are. Museum artifacts may be created by people as part of their life, whether wampum belts, furniture, utensils, or equipment, or they can be natural objects such as fossils and scientific samples. Museum collections are created as research and study collections, for exhibition, and for public programming.

The bibliographic or descriptive tools used to provide access to library, archives, and museum materials have some commonalities and some clear differences. At the most basic level, each profession develops access tools to ensure that staff and users can locate relevant information. Libraries have a significantly longer tradition of cataloging and providing access, and they have accepted a clearly stated set of purposes for library catalogs as defined in the Paris Principles.[16] The archival profession has not explicitly agreed upon a statement of principles for archival "catalogs," finding aids, or other access tools. An increasingly standardized set of methods has developed for catalog records and finding aids, propelled predominantly by the introduction of automated approaches and the consequent need for consistency and predictability.[17] Museum access is the most complicated of the three, as it is in a more protean stage at this time. Most museum collections were created to support internal institutional research and exhibition needs, not to provide primary sources for public study and research. Although some museums share their research collections in a more public manner, it has not been a primary mission. Efforts are underway, but professional standards for cataloging/description or access in museums have not been established.[18]

A repository may hold a combination of these materials and may face the challenge of providing appropriate access to all three in some related way. Simply using one set of descriptive principles on all three types will ultimately limit accessibility to and comprehensibility of the resources. Some efforts have been made to provide "seamless" access to combined materials, but a standardized, accepted approach to integrating catalogs or Web sites for materials with different control issues has not been achieved or even widely discussed across professions.

---

16 *Statement of Principles adopted at the International Conference on Cataloging Principles,* Paris 1961, annotated and edited with commentary and examples by Eva Verona, et al. (London: IFLA Committee on Cataloguing, 1971). The principles include supporting collocation so that all known editions of an item can be located, collocation that enables all items on a topic to be located, and known item identification supporting location of all items by an author or a particular work by an author.

17 The development of the MARC Format, for use with archives and manuscripts, and EAD, are examples of standardized approaches resulting from the introduction of automation to archival access. MARC and EAD are described in more detail in chapter 3.

18 A useful brief summary of museum practices can be found in Richard Rinehart, "Cross-Community Applications: The EAD in Museums," in *Encoded Archival Description on the Internet,* ed. Wendy Duff and Daniel Pitti (New York: Haworth Press, 2001).

When Are Archival Arrangement and Description Practices Appropriate?

Staff members in manuscript libraries, historical societies, university archives, and other organizations with "historical materials" some-times express confusion about when to use archival approaches to their holdings. In fact, they may have collections that include a mix-ture of materials, some requiring library cataloging, others archival description, and yet others museum cataloging.

With the advent of automated access, many archivists began to use the term *archival control* to indicate when materials should be approached using archival techniques. This concept essentially explains that a body of materials is described archivally, not because of its format or age, but because "its primary and most significant

The Nicholson Family Papers (MSS 219) showing items that are often part of collec-tions of personal papers—correspondence, photographs, postcards, and memora-bilia. Photograph courtesy The Historic New Orleans Collection, Jan White Brantley photographer.

defining characteristic is that it is evidence of the activity for or by which it was created, assembled, or collected."[19]

Simply having something "old" does not make it archival—and something quite new can definitely be archival because it provides evidence of a person or organization's activities. Questions most often arise about whether or when "special formats," such as

Archives are not just "old records."

maps, oral histories, photographs, or electronic media, are archival. By applying the basic concept that the material must provide "evidence of the activity for or by which it was created, assembled, or collected," decisions can be made about the applicability of archival practice.

Maps and photographs, for example, are often found in historical records repositories. But if those maps or photographs are simply "old" or have been kept because of their informational value on topics that are the focus of a repository's collecting area, they are not necessarily archival. They are only archival, and require archival description, if they were created by some person or organization in the process of carrying out daily life or business. So, the Rensselaer County Historical Society's collection of individual "old" maps and atlases for that county can be described according to library practice for published maps. However, the historical society also holds a series of survey maps created for the Glass Lake Owners' Association to define property ownership lines. These are described using archival principles because they were created together in the process of fulfilling a function of the association.

The Relationship of the Arrangement and Description Function to the Institutional Context and Users

While the core principles and practices of archival arrangement and description provide a common foundation for this function, the nature and mission of the records-holding organization will influence implementation. In some cases, particularly for archives, the mission

---

19 Michael Fox, e-mail to Committee on Archival Information Exchange Listserv, 1996.

of the archival collection is to support the parent organization and supply its institutional memory. For others, such as a university archives or research library, the archives or manuscripts collection functions as part of the overall mission to support scholarly research. In yet other cases, perhaps a county historical society or a public library special collection, the mission is service to the general public. Each mission will lead to the high prioritization of certain users, so that access tools developed will address their particular informational needs. This will affect the extent of descriptive work and the types of products developed by arrangement and description.

For example, the University of California library systems have developed a strong resource for scholarly researchers by creating Encoded Archival Description (EAD) finding aids in the *Online Archive of California*.[20] This tool gives potential users substantial information on the records creator and contents through detailed finding aids that provide searchable contextual information, content information, container/folder lists, and some item-level descriptions and selected digitized images. The Ohio Historical Society provides finding aids but also facilitates access for primary user groups, like genealogists, by developing special access tools such as its *Ohio Death Certificate Index*.

Any descriptive program should take into account several questions cogently posed in the *Report of the Canadian Subject Indexing Working Group:*

- Who uses the archives?
- What do users want?
- Why do users want it?
- How do users go about getting it?[21]

The answers to those questions can significantly affect the nature of archival arrangement and description. They will influence the types of access tools provided, the level of description, type of subject, topic, or provenance-based access provided, and the delivery methods, such as published guides, on-line catalogs, or encoded finding aids.

---

20 *Online Archive of California,* available at http:// www.oac.cdlib.org/.
21 *Subject Indexing for Archives: Report of the Subject Indexing Working Group* (Ottawa: Bureau of Canadian Archivists, 1995): 5.

The South Carolina Department of Archives and History research room. Here, collection arrangement and description practices are put to the test daily by researchers. PHOTOGRAPH COURTESY THE SOUTH CAROLINA DEPARTMENT OF ARCHIVES AND HISTORY.

CHAPTER 3

The Context of Arrangement and Description

Development of Archival Practice

European Origins

Although archival practice can be identified among some of the earliest civilizations in the Middle East, modern archival practice in the United States and Canada traces its roots to developments in Europe.[22] The core concepts serving as the foundations of arrangement and description were formalized in the nineteenth century. Following the French Revolution, the first centralized national archives was created in France, and efforts there to manage the voluminous records of government led to the development of the principle of *respect des fonds*. German archivists, similarly struggling with a burgeoning bureaucracy, contributed the concept of original order that, in tandem with the principle of provenance (together essentially approximating the principle of *respect des fonds*), provided a firm foundation for descriptive practice.

Respect des fonds is the principle that the records created, accumulated, and/or maintained and used by an organization or individual must be kept together in their original order, if it exists or has been maintained, and not be mixed or combined with the records of another individual or corporate body.

22 For information on early archival developments, see Ernst Posner, *Archives in the Ancient World,* Archival Classics Series (Chicago: Society of American Archivists, 2002).

An influential manual codifying the practice of archival arrangement and description, the *Manual for the Arrangement and Description of Archives,* was published by three Dutch archivists, Samuel Muller, J. A. Feith, and R. Fruin.[23] Their manual, in addition to clearly defining the role of provenance and original order, drew attention to the need to describe collective groups rather than individual items because of the "organic" nature of archival records, and because of the importance of their relationship to other documents in the filing systems in which they were maintained. Further, they emphasized that archival records result from the functions or activities of an organization and as such need to be described within that context. This manual, translated into English in 1940 by A. J. F. Van Laer, had significant impact on archivists at the u.s. National Archives who set forth many of the essential practices later adopted by American archivists.

British archival traditions also contributed to the development of archives in North America, particularly in Canada. Sir Hilary Jenkinson stressed the importance of archives preserving the "sanctity of evidence" represented by official records and the need for archives to serve the administrative functions of government. The procedures he defined for the registry system, as described in *A Manual of Archival Administration,* were instrumental in the development of practice at the u.s. National Archives and the National Archives of Canada.[24]

Developments in the United States

In the United States, practices for handling manuscripts developed earlier and separately from those for archival records. Justin Winsor, a historian who became both president of the American Library Association and librarian at Harvard, developed the first documented cataloging rules for manuscripts for the Massachusetts Historical Society in 1888. Subsequent developments in cataloging and describing manuscripts followed library traditions, particularly relying on the Library of Congress's Manuscript Division for leadership.[25] Those

---

23 Samuel Muller, J. A. Feith, and R. Fruin, *Manual for the Arrangement and Description of Archives,* 2nd ed., translated by Arthur Levitt, with new introductions by Peter Horsman, Eric Ketelaar, Theo Thomassen, and Marjorie Barritt, Archival Classics Series (Chicago: Society of American Archivists, 2003).

24 Hilary Jenkinson, *A Manual of Archival Administration* (London: P. Land, Humphries, 1937).

25 See Victoria Irons Walch's useful "Chronology of Key Developments in the Evolution of Standards for Archival Description," *American Archivist* 52 (Fall 1989): 441–50.

Tom Owen, founder of the Alabama Department of Archives and History, working with records in the first Archives Office at the state capitol, ca. 1910. PHOTOGRAPH COURTESY ALABAMA DEPARTMENT OF ARCHIVES AND HISTORY.

practices focused on item-level cataloging and analysis and the use of card catalogs for access that paralleled the emerging bibliographic description practices for books. By 1950, however, the Library of Congress developed a new cataloging manual that focused on collection-level description and created "registers" for those collections, while continuing such standard library practices as subject indexing.

Developments in public archives in the early 1900s were promoted by professional historians, taking leadership from the American Historical Association's Public Archives Commission. The first state archives, the Alabama Department of Archives and History, was established in 1901, with the National Archives being founded even later, in 1934. With the immediate challenge of an incredible backlog and massive quantities of modern records, the European practices of provenance and original order provided important tools for arrangement and description practices. The primary tool for access developed by the National Archives was the descriptive inventory for large aggregations termed "record groups," which generally equated to the records of agencies, bureaus, or commissions. State and local governments often adopted the approaches of the National Archives, preferring the descriptive inventory and access based on provenance. This required substantive knowledge on the part of archivists regarding the functions, activities, and history of agencies in order to assist users whose requests included the need for information on topics, locations, people, and organizations. For many years, subject indexing was considered inappropriate for government records.

The two traditions continued, and well into the 1970s, archivists and manuscripts librarians maintained that their approaches must be different due to the nature of the materials they managed. Manuscripts libraries, however, as evidenced by the 1950 Library of Congress cataloging manual, were feeling the increasing pressure of modern manuscripts collections and the need to describe "aggregations" employing the principles of provenance and original order. Archives, conversely, were feeling the inadequacy of the inventory accessible by provenance alone as a tool for meeting the needs of users. The divergent attitudes changed slowly but sufficiently so that by 1977, the Society of American Archivists was able to publish David B. Gracy II's manual, *Archives and Manuscripts: Arrangement and Description,* and other manuals based on modern principles were written specifically for the manuscripts community.[26]

The Movement Toward Standardizing Archival Arrangement and Description

A sea of change in archival arrangement and description came with the introduction of the computer as a tool for access and retrieval. In the 1960s, the Library of Congress led the library community into the world of automated cataloging, developing the MAchine Readable Cataloging (MARC) Format to support shared cataloging. Archival efforts were more limited and dispersed. In 1967, the Council on Library Resources gave a grant to a group of nine institutions to develop SPINDEX II. Those institutions included Cornell University, Minnesota Historical Society, the National Archives, the Smithsonian Institution, and the State Historical Society of Wisconsin. The

---

26 Ruth Bordin and Robert M. Warner, *The Modern Manuscript Library* (New York: Scarecrow Press, 1966) and Kenneth Duckett, *Modern Manuscripts: A Practical Manual for their Management, Care, and Use* (Nashville, Tenn.: American Association for State and Local History, 1975).

National Historical Publications and Records Commission's National Guide Project employed SPINDEX to produce the Directory of Archival Repositories, published in 1978. The National Archives ceased its involvement in the development and use of SPINDEX II in 1973. Others continued to use SPINDEX, but developed individual implementations that were not compatible.[27]

The introduction of automation into archival repositories beginning in the 1970s underscored the need for common practices and standards. That need became especially evident during the 1980s. The Society of American Archivists convened the National Information System Task Force (NISTF) in 1977 to consider what kind of national information system to support— the most likely options initially appearing to be the *National Union Catalog of Manuscript Collections* (NUCMC) or the NHPRC's National Guide Project.

Automation underscored the need for descriptive standards.

Discussions turned soon, however, to the need for a common set of data elements, commonly understood to be developed as the foundation of archival description to facilitate information exchange. As part of its work, NISTF asked Elaine Engst of Cornell University to compare the data elements used in a wide range of manuscript and archival repositories. The resulting *Data Elements Dictionary* developed for NISTF in 1980 clearly demonstrated that the perceived differences in practice between archives and manuscripts were not as pronounced as previously portrayed and presented very surmountable obstacles.[28]

NISTF then sought to either develop or identify an existing data elements structure that could be adopted by the archival community for exchange of archival descriptive information. Substantive practical issues surrounded this effort. The development and maintenance of a standard for data exchange is by no means insubstantial. As NISTF learned, the Library of Congress took responsibility for managing the MARC Format, with advice from the library community. The staff and

---

27 H. Thomas Hickerson, *Archives & Manuscripts: An Introduction to Automated Access,* Basic Manual Series (Chicago: Society of American Archivists, 1981); Stephen E. Hannestad, "Clay Tablets to Micro Chips: The Evolution of Archival Practice into the Twenty-First Century," *Library Hi Tech* 9, no. 4 (1991). SPINDEX was implemented by a number of other archives including the Delaware Hall of Records, the Kentucky Department of Libraries and Archives, the South Carolina Department of Archives and History, and the Washington State Archives.

28 Elaine Engst, "Data Elements Dictionary," in MARC *for Archives and Manuscripts: The* AMC *Format,* by Nancy Sahli (Chicago: Society of American Archivists, 1985).

resources needed for such work went beyond what the archival community could conceive of supporting, and the National Archives did not play a comparable role in the archival community to that of the Library of Congress in the library community.

In addition, developing a standard for data exchange was only the beginning. Software would need to be developed to support archives using the data exchange standard—and the small size and relative poverty of the archival community did not bode well for the possibility of any adequate software being developed. The archival community had already experienced difficulties in attempting to create and use SPINDEX II as common software for archival descriptive access.

NISTF therefore recommended that the archival community join forces with the library community and adapt the MARC Format for Manuscripts into a more viable format for archives and manuscripts.[29] The task force, particularly with involvement of its director, David Bearman, worked closely with the Library of Congress to develop a more viable format for archival materials. This format revision, renamed the MARC Format for Archives and Manuscript Control (MARC AMC), provided a much more usable set of data elements.

Although MARC brought with it a number of complications, it provided a solid basis on which the u.s. archival community could begin its foray into automated access. Since many archives and manuscripts collections are located in a library setting, the ability to share a catalog or software with that library was important in providing the wherewithal to begin automated archival access. The Research Libraries Group (RLG) took a leadership role in urging archival institutions to contribute their records to the Research Libraries Information Network (RLIN), a bibliographic information resource created initially by research libraries.[30]

The introduction of the MARC AMC format in 1983 and the possibility for exchange of information, participation in library systems, and national utilities were major catalysts for organizations to develop standardized practices. MARC AMC was instrumental in putting to rest the former notion that archival descriptive practices in the United States could not be codified into any common guidelines or standards

---

29 The Library of Congress developed the initial MARC Format for Manuscripts, but it proved to be suited primarily to small or literary manuscripts collections. Only a few repositories implemented it.

30 RLG is currently international in its membership including over 163 research libraries, archival repositories, and special libraries.

applicable to a wide range of institutions, and particularly to both archives and manuscripts. While it was and remains an imperfect solution to the multidimensional, multilevel needs of archival description, the dissemination and adoption of

———————————
MARC provided a data exchange standard for archives.
———————————

MARC AMC was critical in bringing about a transformation in the standardization of archival description. The archival profession finally was developing common terminology, common practices, and common retrieval alternatives to support the needs of its users.

Almost simultaneously, the Library of Congress published the first version of *Archives, Personal Papers, and Manuscripts* (APPM) by Steven L. Hensen in 1983, because chapter 4 of the existing *Anglo-American Cataloguing Rules 2* (AACR2) was not functional for archival practice.[31] The manual provided archivists in the U.S. with the first set of clear rules for creating the content of archival descrip-

———————————
APPM provided a content standard for U.S. archivists.
———————————

tions. The first edition focused predominantly on manuscripts collections, with the second edition expanded to incorporate governmental and organizational records issues. The development of this manual provided an essential tool for guiding the standardization of the content that was placed in the MARC AMC data elements. Its structure and content, parallel to that of AACR2, assisted archivists to integrate their descriptive information with that of libraries, and allowed many archives to take advantage of existing on-line library public access catalogs. By following common rules, archivists were able to become more involved in the larger "information access" systems of many university, public, and state libraries.

This period of attention to archival description also resulted in the development in the U.S. of several manuals focused on standardizing practice for particular forms of material (e.g., graphic materials, moving images, oral histories), as well as the adoption of controlled vocabularies, thesauri, and other indexing tools. (See discussion of professional standards in chapter 4.)

As availability of Internet access spread in the 1990s, archivists began to mount finding aids, first on gopher sites and then in HTML. As discussion of standardizing practice began, archivists recalled the

---

31 The *Anglo-American Cataloguing Rules 2* serves as the standard cataloging rules for the library community.

Zhou Xiaomu, a Ph.D. student in the School of Information at the University of Michigan, processes a collection at the Bentley Historical Library.

divergent approaches that had arisen with SPINDEX. The U.S. archival community focused attention on the Berkeley Finding Aid Project developed by the University of California library systems to create a standardized approach to presenting finding aids on the Internet by employing encoding standards that are independent of hardware and software constraints. While the initial goal focused on the university network in California, the participants hoped to develop an approach that would allow for universal access to descriptions internationally.

Led by Daniel Pitti of the University of California at Berkeley, project participants considered a range of encoding techniques, finally determining that Standardized General Markup Language (SGML NISO 8879) was the most flexible option. The subsequent development of the Encoded Archival Description document type definition (EAD DTD) involved a series of collaborative research projects and meetings among representatives from a range of archival repositories and professional organizations. Attention was given to ensuring that the standard and associated documents were user-friendly, and the Research Libraries Group developed a basic workshop that the Society of American Archivists subsequently assumed responsibility for offering.[32]

---

32 Janice E. Ruth, "The Development and Structure of the Encoded Archival Description

The Library of Congress Network Development/MARC Standards Office agreed to become the maintenance agency for EAD and to help furnish technical guidance to institutions encoding finding aids. The Society of American Archivists remained responsible for ongoing oversight of the intellectual contents of the EAD standard. A tag library and application guidelines are available, along with a Web site that offers assistance and information both on encoding and on software and hardware issues.[33] EAD has been adopted by a range of institutions internationally, and is being used by a number of consortial projects.[34]

In 2000, the Canada-U.S. Taskforce on Archival Description (CUS-TARD) undertook a collaborative effort to reconcile the two North American archival descriptive standards (*APPM* and *RAD*) with their international counterparts, *ISAD(G)* and *ISAAR(CPF)*. The initial intent was to develop a single standard for use in both countries. A draft document was completed, but the task force found it was unable to sufficiently accommodate divergent practices and approaches in the two countries. The effort did, however, bring practice in closer alignment in many areas, as reflected in the two resulting standards, *Describing Archives: A Content Standard* in the United States and *Rules for Archival Description 2* in Canada.

Developments in Canada

Through the 1980s and 1990s, the move toward standardizing arrangement and description was also underway in Canada, although archivists there took a different approach. The Canadians determined that it was preferable to begin with the establishment of standardized descriptive practice, then move to its automation. In 1984, the Canadian Working Group on Archival Descriptive Standards

RAD provided descriptive standards for the Canadian archival community.

(EAD) Document Type Definition," in *Encoded Archival Description on the Internet*, ed. Wendy Duff and Daniel Pitti (New York: Haworth Press, 2001).

33 Society of American Archivists, *Encoded Archival Description Tag Library, 2002* (Chicago: Society of American Archivists, 2003); ibid., *Encoded Archival Description Application Guidelines, Version 1.0* (Chicago: Society of American Archivists, 1999); Society of American Archivists EAD Roundtable Web site available at http://jefferson.village.virginia.edu/ead/.

34 International users include University of Liverpool Special Collections, University of Glasgow Archives & Business Records Centre, Australian War Memorial, and the Public Records Office (United Kingdom). Examples of consortial projects include the Online Archive of California, Texas Archival Resources Online, American Heritage Virtual Archive Project, and the North Carolina ECHO Project (Exploring Cultural Heritage Online).

surveyed Canadian archives to obtain a comprehensive overview of types of finding aids created. Its work culminated in the report, *Toward Descriptive Standards.*[35] As a result of that report, the Bureau of Canadian Archivists (BCA) created the Planning Committee for Descriptive Standards (PCDS) to plan and coordinate the effort to develop descriptive standards for Canadian archivists. The PCDS included representation from the Association des archivists du Québec, the Association of Canadian Archivists, the Bureau of Canadian Archivists, and an observer from the National Archives. Working groups developed general rules as well as those focusing on specific media. The work of the PCDS resulted in the *Rules for Archival Description* (RAD), a manual that provides specific guidelines for description of different formats of material.[36] A careful process of training in the use of RAD and a process for maintaining the standard provided strong support for ensuring its use in the Canadian archival community.

RAD differed from the U.S. approach in that it did not prescribe any particular finding aids or products (such as the U.S. MARC AMC "catalog record"), nor did it endorse any particular data structure. Rather, RAD provided guidance and rules for developing the content of data elements for a range of format types found in archives. The data elements were standardized to allow their use in a variety of descriptive tools. RAD does not define which data elements a finding aid should contain, but it identifies a minimum set of data elements necessary for describing archival records at each level of description.

As noted previously, a revised version, the *Rules for Archival Description,* Second Edition, has been developed. Unlike the earlier RAD, which included media-specific chapters, this edition is organized by descriptive elements and types of descriptive content, and it provides guidance on specific media as part of element rules. It also has more structural and content compatibility with the *ISAD(G): General International Standard Archival Description,* and the *ISAAR(CPF): International Standard Archival Authority Record for Corporate Bodies, Persons and Families* (discussed below).

---

35 Bureau of Canadian Archivists, *Toward Descriptive Standards: Report and Recommendations of the Canadian Working Group on Archival Descriptive Standards* (Ottawa: BCA, 1985).

36 Ibid., *Rules for Archival Description* (Ottawa: BCA, 1990, revised 2001).

Figure 3-1 ISAD(G) Elements of Description

Identity statement area:
 Reference codes
 Title
 Date(s)
 Level of description
 Extent and medium of the unit of description (quantity, bulk, or size)
Context area:
 Name of creator(s)
 Administrative/biographical history
 Archival history
 Immediate source of acquisition or transfer
Content and structure area:
 Scope and content
 Appraisal, destruction, and scheduling information
 Accruals
 System of arrangement
Conditions of access and use area:
 Conditions governing access
 Conditions governing reproduction
 Language/scripts of material
 Physical characteristics and technical requirements
 Finding aids
Allied materials area:
 Existence and location of originals
 Existence and location of copies
 Related units of description
 Publication area
Notes area:
 Note
Description control area:
 Archivist's note
 Rules or conventions
 Date(s) of description

International Efforts to Standardize Description

In the 1980s, the standardization of descriptive practice was also a pervasive archival concern beyond North America. The International Council on Archives (ICA) held an Invitational Meeting of Experts on Descriptive Standards in 1988, which concluded that descriptive standards were a major priority. Consequently, the ICA established the Ad Hoc Commission on Descriptive Standards to develop rules for archival description that are internationally applicable. The commission's first product was a set of general principles, the *Statement of Principles Regarding Archival Description,* intended to provide the essential theoretical grounding for description.[37] This was followed by the development of the *ISAD(G): General International Standard Archival Description,* providing a set of general principles to underpin archival description and a basic set of data elements and rules for description.[38] The ICA was especially concerned about creating an international standard to provide a common structure for archives in developing countries that lack the professional infrastructure to be developing descriptive standards individually. This was followed in 1996 by the Ad Hoc Commission's development of the *ISAAR(CPF): International Standard Archival Authority Record for Corporate Bodies, Persons and Families,* a standard designed to provide guidance in the creation of contextual and authority records for archives.[39]

> **The ICA developed *ISAD(G)* to provide an international standard for description.**

---

37 International Council on Archives, *Statement of Principles Regarding Archival Description* (Ottawa: ICA), 1992.

38 Ibid., ISAD(G).

39 Ibid., ISAAR(CPF): *International Standard Archival Authority Record for Corporate Bodies, Persons and Families* (Ottawa: ICA, 1996).

CHAPTER 4

The Practice of Arrangement and Description

Overview

This section will review the practices, standards, and issues relating to each step in the process of arrangement and description. While the steps may vary somewhat according to different groups of records or individual institutional or personal work styles, they are the essential components for ensuring appropriate arrangement and description that will result in well-developed finding aids, on-line catalogs, special indexes, and similar tools.

Accessioning Archival Records

The goal of accessioning is to establish initial control over a group of records. That control needs to be accomplished for administrative, physical care, and access purposes. Archivists must invest the time necessary for this initial stage of work, as it can be used to inform decisions regarding additional steps to be taken and to establish the priority for future descriptive work on the records.

Accessioning provides initial control over records.

Figure 4-1 Steps in Archival Arrangement and Description

Accessioning archival records
- Undertake physical and administrative transfer of records
- Review the general content and condition of the records
- Create initial control tools
- Assess future needs for arrangement, description, and preservation

Establishing contextual information for arrangement and description
- Identify relevant information on the person or organization responsible for creating, accumulating, maintaining, or using the records
- Identify the function or roles records were created to support
- Identify recordkeeping practices that may be evidenced in the records
- Identify significant events or developments to which the records relate

Arranging the records
- Identify or provide a physical arrangement for the records
- Identify the intellectual relationships and arrangement of the records

Physically processing the records
- Rehouse records as necessary
- Identify preservation needs
- Separate fragile or special format records
- Weed extraneous materials
- Note informational content

Describing the records
- Determine the level of description to provide for the group of records
- Describe the core identifying elements of information
- Describe the contextual information
- Describe the physical characteristics
- Describe the informational content
- Provide access points/index terms
- Describe the administrative information needed to support use

Developing access tools
- Create a finding aid to the records
- Develop additional access tools
- Disseminate access tools

Undertake Physical and Administrative Transfer of Records

During appraisal and acquisition, records of permanent value are identified. The actual transfer of those records may take place soon after, or it may wait for years. A group of records may be transferred as a complete group, or it may be given to the archives or manuscripts repository in stages as the donor or organization no longer has an active need for each portion of the records.

Institutional records are, or should be, regularly identified as archival during the records-management scheduling process. This should result in a regular time frame for transferring records to the archives. Such a schedule generally relates to when the organization no longer actively needs to use the records for legal, fiscal, or administrative purposes. The time for transfer to the archives is identified in a records schedule. At that point, appropriate documentation needs to be signed to verify that the records are officially and legally being placed in the custody of the archives and identifying any special restrictions or conditions.

Beth Golding surveys records prior to transfer. Records sometimes have physical conditions that pose special challenges for accessioning. PHOTOGRAPH COURTESY FLORIDA BUREAU OF ARCHIVES AND RECORDS MANAGEMENT.

With personal records or manuscripts, arrangements for transfer are subject to more direct negotiations with the donor. Records sometimes will be donated in their entirety, but they may also be transferred in groups over time. Again, formal legal donor agreements are essential to establish the right of an archives to have custody, as well as to provide the conditions for administering that group of records, particularly with relationship to their literary copyright and use.[40]

---

40 For a sample donor agreement, see *Sample Forms for Archival and Records Management Programs* (Chicago: Society of American Archivists and ARMA International, 2002).

Figure 4-2 Records Schedule

Clemson University Records Schedule

Vice Provost for Academic Affairs
Dean of Agriculture, Forestry and Life Sciences

CU-VPAA-AS-AD-AE-AWO-5

Record of Evaporation and Climatological Observations

Description:
Contains weather data from various weather stations in South Carolina.
Information includes daily high and low temperature, supplemental read-
ings, amount of precipitation, wind anemometer dial readings, evapora-
tion, and remarks. This information is also available through the Clemson
University computer systems.

Retention: 5 years in laboratory
University Archives: Permanent
Schedule approved 12/21/1990

The transfer of records is not simply a legal step to be accomplished, however. The donor or transferring organization often has a
wealth of knowledge that can be essential in the later stages of arrangement and description. If background information on the creator, use,
and *arrangement* or filing structure of the records was not elicited as
part of the appraisal and acquisition process, this is a critical opportunity to ask those questions.

In some cases, the actual group of records transferred, donated, or
purchased and then brought into legal custody by accessioning may
not be the grouping in which the records are finally described. During
the arrangement process, the archivist may discover that, based on

provenance and original order, the *accession* is really two or more groups of records that need to be described separately. This can happen when records become disorganized over time or are kept poorly by an individual or organization.

The physical transfer of records may take place in a variety of ways. Ideally, records will be boxed in the office, home, or storage location with care and attention to preserving the original arrangement and manner in which the records were kept. A box/folder list prepared by the creating organization or individual may provide clear evidence of the record groupings and relationships. In an unfortunate number of cases, particularly with the personal papers of a decedent, the boxes have been packed with few clues to the way in which they were maintained or used. To avoid this, archival staff should undertake the packing of boxes for transfer when possible to preserve useful information from the records location. When that is not possible, the individual or group who will be preparing records for transfer should be given information on how to minimize the "dumping stuff into boxes" effect. (See appendix B for examples of the arrangement process.)

> **The archivist should pack up records whenever possible—there are important clues for arrangement.**

Review the General Content and Condition of the Records

After records have physically arrived at the archives, a very preliminary review needs to take place for several purposes. First, the records need to be assessed for physical care and storage issues. Some materials in the records, such as nitrate negatives, audiotapes, computer tapes or disks, or fragile items, may need to be segregated for alternate storage because of special needs or problems they pose. As a precaution, any records that may have physical problems, such as dampness, pest infestation, or mold, should be kept in a separate area until they can be assessed. The archivist needs to avoid bringing preservation problems into an area where those problems may affect other records. In addition to serious preservation threats that transferred records pose, archivists have been known to encounter the random peanut butter sandwich, whiskey bottle, or box of chocolates.

An accrual or accretion is an addition to the existing series or manuscript group. It contains records that had not been transferred previously, but are part of the same group based on provenance.

> An *accrual* or *accretion* is an addition to the existing series or manuscript group. It contains records that had not been transferred previously, but are part of the same group based on provenance.

In addition, the initial review provides a useful opportunity to identify problems needing to be addressed in arrangement and description, including disarranged or unarranged records, the existence of copies or extraneous material that can be weeded, poorly identified records, and gaps or missing records. An accession can be an entire manuscript group or record series, or it may be only a portion of the entire body of records. Particularly in the case of organizational records, it can be an accretion to records that have already been placed in the repository.[41] This can happen, though less frequently, with personal or family records as well. An accrual (accretion) should not be treated as a separate description, but integrated into the existing descriptive tools. The archivist should update those tools to reflect the accrual, rather than creating a separate set of descriptive tools.

Create Initial Access and Control Tools

Once the records arrive at the archives it is essential to establish an accession file documenting the transfer information. A surprising number of institutions have not maintained this kind of information in the past. Without such information, they are subject to significant problems in administering access to the records in light of increasing concerns over copyright, not to mention their ability to prove legal ownership of the records. Some archives also maintain an accession register or log as a summary tool for controlling new acquisitions.[42]

> An accession file is an internal resource for documenting the legal transfer of records to an archives. It contains documents giving proof of custody and information on donors. It should never be given to researchers to review.

---

41 The ISAD(G) uses the term *accrual* rather than *accretion*.
42 See *Sample Forms for Archival and Records Management Programs.*

Figure 4-3 Example of Manuscript Group and Subsequent Accrual

Summary description of papers
[Donated by Anna K. Cunningham (sister) in 1990.]
Mary E. Cunningham Papers, 1940–1970.
This collection contains a wide variety of material that relates to the professional life of Mary E. Cunningham. Included are various records relating to Cunningham's service at the New York State Historical Association. These include correspondence, publications and periodicals, memoranda concerning program development, and material relating to her editorship of "New York History." Also included are a number of files relating to Cunningham's activities in the development of educational programs about New York State History including material relating to the filmstrip series "Our York State" and her newspaper article of the same title. This material includes manuscripts of articles, clippings of the article, and correspondence.

Accrual donated by her sister, Anna K. Cunningham, in 1993
Professional material relates to Cunningham's service in the Kennedy administration, her work at Rand McNally publishing, and her activities in the Democratic party. Also included are personal and family items including photos, Cunningham's resumé, her transcripts from Cornell University, and letters from family members.

Revised summary description integrating the 1993 accrual
Mary E. Cunningham Papers, 1940–1970.
This collection contains a wide variety of material that relates to the personal and professional life of Mary E. Cunningham. Included are various records relating to Cunningham's service at the New York State Historical Association.

The italicized sentences shows the information added to the original description to reflect the accrual.

Personal and family items include photos, Cunningham's resumé, her transcripts from Cornell University, and letters from family members. Professional items include correspondence, publications and periodicals, memoranda concerning program development, and material relating to her editorship of "New York History." Also included are a number of files relating to Cunningham's activities in the development of educational programs about New York State History including material relating to the filmstrip series "Our York State" and her newspaper article of the same title. This material includes manuscripts of articles, clippings of the article, and correspondence. *Other professional materials relate to Cunningham's service in the Kennedy administration, her work at Rand McNally publishing, and her activities in the Democratic party.*

Figure 4-4 Sample Accession Log

Date Rec'd	Accession Number	Office of Origin/ Source	Donor	Title	Quantity	Location

As archives increasingly automate various functions, archivists need to consider whether they will maintain a separate accession log in either automated or paper form. Archivists are increasingly considering the value of entering information at the accession level into the on-line public access catalog. This allows both staff and external users to know the full holdings of the archives immediately, even if at a preliminary level.

The accessioning stage is a good time to create a simple summary description. Because few repositories have the staffing and resources to fully describe records immediately upon receiving them, accessioning offers the opportunity to construct a simple initial arrangement and description that allows basic access until records can be fully described. Descriptive information collected at the point of accessioning should be brief and reflect the entirety of records transferred or donated. That may take the form of a simple summary as provided in figure 4-5.

Some institutions may elect to fully develop the descriptive tools immediately. In this case, the specific practices, elements of information, and standards referenced on pages 71–97 should be implemented. A repository may handle all of its accessions this way, or only those of particular value or immediate interest.

More frequently, the archivist may use a "blunt" level of descriptive control at the accessioning stage. This will involve determining basic elements of information such as identifying the creating organization or individual, assigning a general title, approximating the date span, estimating quantity, and perhaps writing a very brief overview of general contents. All of these can be based on information readily available

Figure 4-5 Accession Description Form

Date rec'd	Accession no.	Location
12/12/1994	13464-94	West Alcove, Range 3, Unit 4, Shelf 6

Creating individual/organization
Charles E. Williams

Title
Papers

Quantity 2 linear feet

Approximate dates 1910—1965

General contents Family letters and school records

Donor/transferring agency Emily Williams Johnson (daughter)

Accessioned by Jack Elder	Date December 15, 1994

at the time the records are received. Later, more thorough contextual background research and description of the records will take place, following the practices discussed subsequently in this manual. This type of "preliminary" descriptive work done during accessioning is useful under several conditions. The archivist may be the first person with training to be given responsibility for an archives or manuscript collection that has been amassed over time. When few or inaccurate finding aids exist, going through the full collection and establishing legal, physical, and initial descriptive control can be beneficial. In other circumstances, an archivist may want to create some initial control until more time can be devoted to to the full descriptive process.

Some institutions do not permit access to records until they have been fully described. Others allow users to review unprocessed papers with supervision. This is an institutional decision that needs to be carefully considered. If the descriptive backlog is so extensive that it

Figure 4-6 Accession Description Form

Date rec'd	Accession no.	Location
12/12/1994	13464-94	West Alcove, Range 1 Shelf 2—3

Creating individual/organization
Katherine Valdez

Title
Synchronized swimming collection

Quantity 15 cubic feet

Approximate dates 1930—1990

General contents Videotapes, photographs, autographs, letters, scrapbooks, various written materials

Donor/transferring agency Professor Katherine Valdez

Accessioned by Kayla Johnson	Date February 21, 1993

Box list

Katherine Valdez Synchronized Swimming Collection		
contents	Box number	Location
Videotapes	1–3	Range 1, Shelf 2
Photographs	4–7	Range 1, Shelf 2
Autographs	8–9	Range 1, Shelf 2
Scrapbooks	10–14	Range 1, Shelf 3
Topical files	15–16	Range 1, Shelf 3

may take years for an institution to complete needed work, then providing some supervised access will allow users to take advantage of records that may be important for their work. Some oversight of researchers using undescribed papers is necessary both for security reasons and to ensure that they do not disturb provenance.

If the full descriptive process is not done at the accessioning stage, likely some adjustments and changes will be made later to the information initially collected. For example, after investigation the archivist may determine that the title or name of the organization or individual creating the group of records may need revision. Dates will usually be made more precise, and differentiations between inclusive dates, *dates of recordkeeping activity,* and bulk dates may be made. (See page 74.) In other cases, the archivist may find that the group of records initially accessioned needs to be arranged into more specific groupings for the purposes of accurate description. When an institution has a considerable backlog or limited staffing, however, having some basic information provides the ability to give access to records, whether for staff or research purposes.

If a records disposition form or an appraisal/acquisitions report exists, some of this information may already be available to expedite the accessioning process. It is also helpful at this point to create a box-level list to assist with physical control and retrieval. The box list, like the accessioning record, provides very basic control and is drawn from the obvious information available at the time records are received.

Assess Future Needs for Arrangement, Description, and Preservation

Because so many manuscripts libraries and archives have more records than they have staff to care for them, establishing priorities for arrangement, description, and preservation is important both to effective use of resources and to making available the records most likely to be in demand. At the point of accessioning, the archivist can benefit from consulting with the person who did the appraisal/acquisition and with the preservation and reference staff to determine priorities for further arrangement and description, and to identify any special access tools that might be useful to develop. If possible, the institution should develop a needs assessment tool or processing plan

The condition in which records arrive may be a determining factor in their retention. Having institutional policies and procedures in place can assist the archivist in making these difficult decisions a little less painful. PHOTOGRAPH COURTESY JAMES MADISON UNIVERSITY.

for records so they can be compared with others awaiting arrangement and description. This assessment can be a collaborative effort between description and reference staff (if indeed they are different!), and it can inform the staff members of issues and directions that affect each function.

Establishing the Context in which Records Were Created

The context in which records were created, managed, assembled, or accumulated is crucial to understanding archives and manuscript records. Archivists commonly understand the value of contextual information for the users of records, but context is also valuable for the archivist undertaking arrangement and description. Important clues to assist in the arrangement and description process can be found during the search for information; these clues provide insight into the functions or personal roles for which

Context provides critical information for both users and for archivists.

records were created and used, as well as the characteristics, directions, priorities, and philosophies of both individuals and organizations. In addition, the historical context in which an organization operated or a person lived provides important background on records practices and significant events or trends that is essential to the accurate arrangement and description of records.

Research Background on the Person or Organization Responsible for Creating, Maintaining, or Using the Group of Records

Gathering information about the person, organization, or group that created, accumulated, assembled, or used a group of records is essential to establishing context. Because archives and manuscript records are exclusively created by human beings, whether as private individuals or those acting in groups and organizations, there is an "attitude" permeating the records. The archivist needs to have a sense of this before arranging and describing records, or may entirely misinterpret or misrepresent both the records themselves and the

Archival records have an "attitude."

information in them. This is not to argue that the archivist should interpret the "meaning" of the records for users based on who created them. Rather, he or she should provide sufficient information on the person or organization to support users' ability to assess the information found in a series or manuscript group.

For example, a user may interpret correspondence relating to the civil rights movement differently if the person who created and used the letters was variously a lawyer, a Communist Party organizer, an African American minister, a southern governor, or a Ku Klux Klan member. While such information may be more obvious if the minister is Martin Luther King, Jr., or the lawyer William Kunstler, the majority of records held by archives and manuscripts collections originated with creators whose names and attitudes are not so well known. Nonetheless, the attitudes and ideas of the less famous can affect the content and character of information just as profoundly. And it can be far more difficult for users to be aware of those subtleties when the creators lacked sufficient prominence or notoriety to leave a solid trail of published evidence. Hence, the archivist plays an important role in providing context.

Additionally, locating some simple identifying information on individuals and organizations can be complicated. The identity of an author who publishes under a range of pseudonyms or who has a common name can confuse both archivist and user. Other personal information such as political or social attitudes and positions may not be clearly evident, but can certainly affect the content of records.

Organizations, particularly in the twentieth century, have a penchant for reorganizing, renaming, merging, and splitting that leaves a web of names and relationships to be untangled. Records from a hospital that has survived a host of mergers will pose interesting challenges in identifying how series continue, split, and change to meet functional and organizational alterations. Like personal philosophies, organizations can also have distinctive political, social, or philosophical positions that users may find important in assessing archival records.

Identify the Function or Roles Records Were Created to Support

One of the *a priori* statements that might be made about archival records is this: they were created for a purpose. The reason may be simple, temporal, convoluted, reprehensible, or even silly, but no person or organization creates records out of the sheer desire to do so. A corollary is that few records creators embed in their records a statement of why they created them or how they used them.

Archival records are created for a *purpose.*

Identifying the functions and activities of organizations can be fairly straightforward since there are laws, regulations, bylaws, mission statements, charters, annual reports, and other bureaucratic documents to provide that information. However, those functions and activities may be altered over time in ways that significantly affect records content and records-keeping practices. In addition, some organizations assume non-mandated functions that may be of particular importance to note.

The purpose for which an individual creates, accumulates, or uses a group of records, such as personal diaries, may be less easily divined. However, the roles and activities that they support are perhaps less uncertain and provide the necessary basis for arrangement and description. For example, in arranging a group of personal papers from a university professor, an archivist might find natural groupings based on her professional affiliations, professorial work, avocations, and family roles. (See appendix C, examples 2 and 3.)

Identify Recordkeeping Practices Evidenced in the Records

Many European nations have records-keeping traditions that involve clearly defined types of records with specific content expectations.[43] In Canada, where there are strong governmental ties to Great Britain's records-keeping tradition, practices align closely with those in Europe. In the United States, however, those record definitions are not so clearly evident particularly in personal records. Nonetheless, certain types or forms of material do have historic characteristics that may be important for the archivist to understand when attempting to arrange and describe archival records.

For example, nineteenth-century accounting practices proscribed very specific types of recordation—waste books, cashbooks, and journals among them. Each of these had very clear purposes, and all were related to one another in a particular system to provide fiscal accountability. Proper arrangement of the records of a nineteenth-century business requires the ability to recognize each of these tools and arrange them to reflect the way they were used in that business. Contextual information on the forms of accounting records is critical to accurately understanding and using them. Archivists may find it necessary to familiarize themselves with the recordkeeping practices of accountants, courts, psychiatric and medical institutions, religious groups, and a myriad of other organizations and professions, as well as learn how they have changed over time. Professional associations frequently have members who are interested in the history

Checking out professional literature in a library, by contacting a professional organization or by talking to a person in that field can help in understanding records keeping practices.

---

43   An excellent example of this is the Dutch records-keeping tradition as described in Peter Sigmond and David Bearman, "Explorations of Form of Material Authority Files by Dutch Archivists," *American Archivist* 50 (Spring 1987): 249–53. Many European nations have tightly defined "records formats" that result from specific functions and are predictable in both content and format. This level of definition is not nearly so predominant in u.s. records-keeping traditions, often to the bafflement of our European colleagues.

and past practices of their profession or interest area, and some research libraries retain books and professional manuals from past eras.

Identify Significant Events or Developments to which the Records Relate

While archives deal increasingly with more recent records, the basic fact remains that most holdings will be of an historical nature. As such, they will reflect mores, attitudes, practices, and actions of a different era. Assessing salient historical contextual information prior to arrangement and description will improve the quality of that work. In the past, when formal archival training was not readily available, the historical context of archives led many organizations to hire historians to fill archival positions. While comprehensive knowledge of the historical period is by no means necessary, the archivist should have a sufficient sense of the period to which records relate and be attuned to particular events or developments that they may reflect.

An archivist describing the records of a mental health institution, for example, needs to be aware of the changing approaches in treatment from homeopathy, to psychosurgery, to drug therapy. This will serve as a base for identifying whether the institution used standard treatments for its time, or whether it was "ahead" or "behind" in its approaches. In some cases, the "nonreaction" in records to a major event may be noteworthy, as in town records from the Revolutionary War era that make no note or show any evidence of being affected by the change from colonial to national government.

The pressure of time, staffing, and the desire to make records available as soon as possible often results in limited attention being given to the background research needed to clearly establish the context in which records were created. Some institutions compile such information as the description process proceeds, drawing from the records for some of that context. Though it is entirely possible to arrange and describe records with little or no contextual information, the resulting arrangement and description is likely to be seriously compromised. Information provided out of context may lead to inaccurate conclusions, cultural misrepresentations, and false statements. The archivist's responsibility to both the records and the user community demands more thorough attention to the role of context in arrangement and description.

Arrangement of Archival Records

Arrangement serves as the initial framework for managing and understanding records. Archives and manuscripts are managed as aggregations both because of their size and the contextual relationship that records have in the grouping in which they were created or used. Archival records must be arranged before they can be described. The pattern and level of arrangement will thus influence the level of description that follows.

Identifying or Providing a Physical Arrangement for Records

The first step archivists generally undertake in addressing arrangement is to review the body of records received to determine what, if any, arrangement already exists. If the records creator is still available to the archivist, that person or organization can readily provide this essential information. If not, which is often the case, then the archivist needs to assess the records as a physical group to identify existing patterns of organization within the records themselves.

For organizational records, this is commonly a less difficult task, since a filing scheme used by the creating office or official to manage the records generally exists. Records are usually created by the organization or by a subdivision of that organization in groupings called *series*. A series is defined as a group of records based on a file system or maintained as a unit because the records result from the same function or activity, have a particular form, or have some other relationship resulting from their creation, accumulation, or use. Some complex records systems may have additional subdivisions, commonly called *subseries*. A series will usually then consist of files or records units, within which individual documents or items are organized. Within the series, records should be kept in the order in which they were created.

> A *series* is a defined group of records based on a file system or maintained as a unit because the records result from the same function or activity, have a particular form, or have some relationship based on their creation.

Figure 4-7 Example of Series and Subseries Within a Group
of Records

National Association of Colored Graduate Nurses Records. 1908–1958.

Series in this group of records include:
- Minutes
- By-Laws and Articles of Incorporation
- Correspondence
  Subseries within this series include:
  - General Correspondence
  - Correspondence on Licensure
  - Correspondence on Discrimination in Hiring
- Speeches and Testimony
- Studies and Reports
- Publications and Printed Materials

Despite the fact that the arrangement should generally be identifiable with organizational records, sometimes records may lack any discernible arrangement. If the organization still exists, the archivist should request that it provide information on what, if any, organizing principle exists. If the organization is defunct, and no pattern for how the records are organized is discernible, then the archivist will need to develop some plan for accomplishing this. Certain resources may prove helpful in developing an arrangement. Professional manuals from the relevant time period may provide evidence of a standard filing system or organization of records. Similarly, a present-day professional in the field may recognize some inherent arrangement or structure to the records that evades the archivist. Rearrangement should only be undertaken after research, careful consideration, and "trying out" the proposed arrangement pattern on a colleague or researcher to assess its merits.

With manuscripts, particularly personal papers, an arrangement may not be inherently obvious, may not have been preserved, or may never have existed. Individuals often carry out their lives and activities in integrated ways and are able to function without great cost if their records are not carefully organized. Nonetheless, people often maintain their personal papers in clusters that reflect their roles or concerns, such as personal financial records, correspondence, school records, and avocational or professional records.

Figure 4-8 Examples of Arrangement Patterns for Family Papers

Family papers organized by family member:
Elder Family Papers, 1840–1920
- Josiah Elder diaries
- Edward Ezra Elder account books
- Elma Elder Nichols correspondence
- George Elder report cards

See additional examples in appendix C.

Family papers organized by material format:
- Henry Mather Hare and Family Fonds, 1863–1944
- Diaries
- Medical records
- Correspondence
- Genealogical charts and notes
- Mather Byles Almon letter book

If personal records do have clear groupings in the way the person or family kept them, those groupings should be maintained. If no existing groupings are evident, a variety of considerations can help to determine how to arrange them. Ease of access and understanding are important to consider before creating an artificial arrangement. With family papers, the archivist may divide the records first by family or family members. Within individual papers, useful groupings might reflect the individual's roles, occupations, interests, or avocations. Depending on the content or nature of the material, arrangement by time period and/or by type of material may make access easier.

Figure 4-9 Arrangement of Sample Records

Charles E. Williams Papers
Organized in two series:
* School and college records, 1907–1930
* World War I letters to and from George Williams, 1916–1917

Hot Coffee, Nevada, Town Clerk's Records
Arranged in three series:
* Town board meeting minutes, 1981–1995
* Election records, 1920–1995
* Registration of births and deaths, 1981–1975

Katherine Valdez Synchronized Swimming Collection

Approaches and alternatives to basic physical arrangement that work for paper records, however, do not readily apply to electronic records. There is not a physical arrangement pattern that can be defined in the same way possible for paper records. Instead, the archivist needs to work with the records creator to identify the records systems within which electronic records function. This focuses attention on how the intellectual relationships among databases or electronic files supported an organization's functions and activities.

Identifying the Intellectual Relationships and Arrangement of Records

Some groups of records, whether organizational series or personal papers, are used entirely on their own without reference to any other body of records. More often, however, groups of records are created, accumulated, assembled, or used in relationship to another series or manuscript group. A complex component of arrangement is to clearly identify how these separate groups of records were created and used by an organization or individual in relationship to each other. Their physical arrangement provides some hints, but contextual information can also provide important clues. Identifying that relationship—

or intellectual arrangement pattern—will assist both potential users and the archivist who undertakes the descriptive work.

A range of possible intellectual arrangement patterns exists. The first is the simple relationship among records of the same creating organization or person. For example, the inmate case files from a state prison have a clear relationship to admission blotters. While each exists as a separate series, the archivist arranging and describing these records needs to be aware of the existence and relationship of these groups of records and later explain that relationship in a finding aid. Similarly, the various groups of records created by a single individual in multiple life roles should be clearly understood by the archivist. Their existence and relationship may be information the user needs. (See figure 4-10.)

The intellectual relationships between records of organizations and those of individuals also need to be understood in the process of arrangement. The records of a leading public figure in the role of an official, for example, will be arranged under the organization for which he or she undertook that role. That person's private or personal papers, however, should be arranged as separate manuscripts records. For example, the records of Booker T. Washington as president of Tuskegee Institute are arranged as as series within the overall records of the Tuskegee pres-

Holmes created this hierarchical scheme for the National Archives, but other institutions found it a practical way to think about the arrangement of their archives also.

ident's office. The writings, correspondence, and family records that resulted from his personal activities, not his work as college president, constitute a manuscript group with its own internal arrangement.[44]

Arrangement has traditionally been seen as a hierarchical scheme, as evidenced in Oliver Wendell Holmes's widely accepted, and often cited, five levels of arrangement devised for the National Archives in the 1940s.[45] The levels he defined were

---

44 In some cases, an official will mix personal and organizational records into one single filing scheme. In such cases, this original provenance should be respected. However, if the individual happened to house his or her personal papers in the same office, but not interfiled into organizational records, then the distinction of organizational and personal records can be followed.

45 Oliver W. Holmes, "Archival Arrangement—Five Different Operations at Five Different Levels," *American Archivist* 27 (January 1964): 21–41. Note that Holmes never put forth his arrangement scheme as reflecting generally applicable principles for all archives. His article clearly states that this was a method developed to manage a serious challenge faced by the National Archives in its early years. While it does provide a useful guide to physical arrangement, the more complicated issues of intellectual arrangement, particularly with multidimensional and multi-agency relationships of records, are not addressed by this scheme.

Figure 4-10 Examples of Complex Records Relationships

Example 1

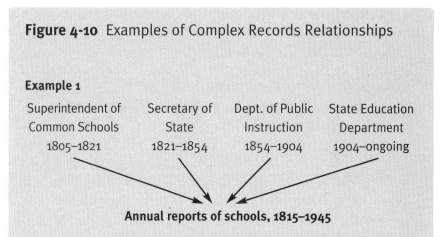

| Superintendent of Common Schools 1805–1821 | Secretary of State 1821–1854 | Dept. of Public Instruction 1854–1904 | State Education Department 1904–ongoing |

Annual reports of schools, 1815–1945

The annual reports are an ongoing series that has been maintained since 1815, but the function of education has been the responsibility of four different departments. The informational nature of the series has not changed, despite changes in the agency responsible for the function. As the responsible agency changed, the records were moved to the next responsible agency. It would be difficult to place this series into a single hierarchy under one record group level.

Example 2

Records of the President are created as a series, merged, then split into separate series as colleges/universities change relationships. Consider the following organizational changes affecting the responsibilities and content of the records for the college/university president over time:

- Baker Bible Institute is founded in 1866.
- Claflin University is founded in 1869.
- Baker Bible Institute and Claflin University are merged into one university (called Claflin University) in 1871.
- Claflin is affiliated with South Carolina State Agricultural and Mechanical Institute from 1875 to 1896.
- The organizations are split apart in 1896 as Claflin University and South Carolina State College, which later becomes South Carolina State University.

- DEPOSITORY: the major divisions or branches of a repository (examples might be divisions based on chronology, material type, or level of government)
- RECORD GROUP OR COLLECTION: the creating agency, organization, individual, or family
- SERIES: documents arranged in accordance with a filing system or maintained as a unit because they result from the same accumulation or filing process, the same function, or the same activity; have a particular form or subject; or because of some other relationship arising out of their creation, receipt, or use
- FILE UNIT: an organized unit of documents grouped together either for current use by the creator or in the process of archival arrangement because they relate to the same subject, activity, or transaction
- DOCUMENT: individual items/units

In the practical application of hierarchical concepts, archivists also find that intellectual arrangement may be multidimensional and multilevel, particularly with modern organizational records, which reflect changing functions or the reorganization or merger of an institution, or with personal records, which document the variety of roles, responsibilities, and interests an individual may pursue. Figure 4-10 provides examples of this.

Archivists need to provide users with a clear understanding of both the physical and intellectual arrangement patterns of records. Explaining those relationships can help researchers identify other manuscripts or records that will either further explain the records they are consulting or provide additional information. It also reflects the actual way in which the records were used in the business or life for which they were created. The arrangement of archives and manuscripts sets the framework for the descriptive work that follows.

Physically Processing the Records

The act of arranging and describing records is not a simple linear process. Once the initial arrangement structure has been established, the archivist turns to the interrelated tasks of physically processing and describing the records. The steps described in this section will likely be undertaken simultaneously with, and provide information for, the actual preparation of descriptive tools. Many of the processes described here can be done by clerical and technical staff or by student interns and volunteers under the supervision of the archivist.

Arranging and describing records is not a simple linear process.

Rehouse Records as Necessary

A basic activity undertaken at this stage if it has not been done already is to provide stable, archival-quality housing by refoldering and reboxing records. Appropriate storage materials are essential, but need not be expensive or "fancy" in design. As records are rehoused, a variety of phased preservation actions may be taken, such as removing paper clips, staples, rubber bands, or other fasteners if they will damage records over time. In some cases, flattening records or interleaving with alkaline paper may be necessary. However, an assessment should be made, preferably in consultation with conservation staff, of the preservation steps that need to be taken with a group of records. Not all records, for example, merit or need interleaving with alkaline paper, and that action can both take up time and resources while significantly expanding the physical space occupied by the records. The sheer extent of modern records especially may make only the most basic rehousing activities practical.

Particular care should be taken with housing provided for special format materials to ensure that they are appropriate for the particular medium of the records. When special format items are integrated into a larger group of records, they may need to be removed for separate storage. In those cases, a separation sheet should be inserted where the removed item was located, both indicating where its intellectual location is and noting where it is physically stored so it can be retrieved for the user.

Special format materials should be properly housed.

Figure 4-11 Potential Activities in Rehousing Records

- Place records in alkaline folders and alkaline boxes.
- Remove rusted paper clips, staples, and rubber bands.
- Flatten folded documents. If a document is too large for a legal-size folder and too valuable to remain folded, transfer it to an oversize box.
- Photocopy newsclippings onto alkaline paper.
- Remove special format materials for storage in appropriate containers. Insert a separation sheet identifying the material and its separate location.
- Remove multiple copies.
- Remove published material (unless it contains hand-annotations) and insert a sheet identifying the published item's bibliographic information.
- Identify any preservation problems (mold, pest infestation, records on unstable media) and remove or segregate records if necessary.
- Always consult with a preservation administrator or conservator for items requiring special containers or storage—these include photographs, video and audiotapes, electronic media, architectural drawings, and oversize maps. Options available change and new technologies provide additional alternatives.

Identify Preservation Needs

Rehousing records presents a good opportunity to note any particular preservation problems. Some issues encountered will require immediate attention, such as bug infestations, mold, unstable media (such as nitrate negatives), or seriously damaged items. Other preservation concerns may not be as time sensitive and can be noted for later attention. If the archives or manuscripts repository has a conservation staff, it is useful to work closely with them to identify the urgency of treatment based not just on the physical condition, but also on the importance of the records. With the limited time and resources available in most archives, the attention of conservation staff should be on treating the most important records for future use.

To avoid problems, boxes should be carefully inspected for potential dangers before they are brought into the repository.

Weed Extraneous Materials

Many archival records are donated or transferred in less than pristine condition. It is not uncommon, particularly with modern records, to find multiple copies of documents, reports, photographs, or publications embedded in the files. There is no sanctity to this multiplicity that necessitates keeping all copies. If annotations exist on the copies or publications, however, there may be a need to keep them. For the truly anxious archivist, two copies at most of multiple items without annotations or intrinsic value can be retained.

Printed publications in particular may be candidates for complete removal, particularly if they are commonly available. For archives that are part of a library, they might be deaccessioned and placed in the library's collection. If the publication appears to be an essential part of the records, a separation sheet might be inserted noting the bibliographic information so a user can identify the item for later reference if relevant.

When items are removed, some deeds of gift/transfer agreements require that the donating person or organization be notified and given the choice of retrieving the materials. In some cases, it may be appropriate to offer the items to a library, or to use them for exhibits or tours. It is not appropriate or ethical for the archivist to either take them for personal use and particularly not to sell or give them away without explicit permission from the donor.

Note Informational Content

As processing takes place, it provides a good opportunity to examine more closely the contents of the records. A set of notes on such things as informational content, changes in recording practices and forms, gaps in dates, significant events, people or topics addressed, and items of particular research value can be noted for later inclusion in the finding aids developed. It is also an opportune time to identify items of particular value for special user groups such as teachers or for exhibit and public programming uses. The information gathered can be used to provide a more effective and specific description.

As records are processed, notes should be made for later description.

Mary Holmes College Archives staff reviewing records for description. Photograph courtesy Evelyn Bonner, Mary Holmes College.

Description of Records

Once records have been arranged, the description can proceed. Using the information gathered in the accessioning and arrangement process, the archivist needs to begin a careful review of the actual records, keeping in mind the context in which those records were created, the archival institution's mission, and the primary users. Depending on the extent and nature of the records, the archivist may not need to examine each individual document, but may rely on information from container/folder lists and review of selected portions to summarize contents. The result of this process will be one or more *finding aids*, the generic term used for a range of access tools developed to provide users with a summary explanation of the records.

Determine the Level of Description to Provide for the Group of Records

Archival description should proceed from the general to the specific. That is, descriptive information should be provided for the broadest aggregation of records (at the group/collection or *fonds* level when appropriate), and when useful, for additional levels (series, subseries, sub-subseries, item). At each level, the core elements of description identified in the next section should be provided.

Description proceeds from the general to the specific.

The descriptive levels should be consistent with the levels of arrangement existing within the records. However, even if records are physically arranged at a more detailed level, it may not always be necessary to provide separate descriptive elements for each level. Based on the potential use and users of a group of records, the archivist needs to determine when it will be useful and productive for access to describe records at each succeeding level. No hard and fast rule can effectively be applied regarding what levels of description to employ beyond the imperative to describe records first at the most general level of aggregation.

The goal of archival description is to ensure access to the records. An increasingly perplexing problem for archivists, especially those with modern records collections, is how to accomplish this with a substantial amount of records and the ever-present problem of insufficient staff resources. Many institutions also have considerable backlogs of undescribed records—sometimes constituting the majority of the institution's holdings. Under these conditions, achieving access can be hampered by focusing on describing all records to the fullest extent. Some archives with large collections or large backlogs begin by describing records at the first level of aggregation (the record group, collection, or series) and proceeding with further description only if records are used frequently or have significant monetary or artifactual value. By providing a core description and a basic container list, access is at least possible. When records sit in unidentified, undescribed boxes on the shelves for years, their value is seriously diminished. Archival description should be an organic process. Records do not need to be described once and for all time. Once a core description is completed, a priority for further description can be determined and the description expanded as researcher demand, resources, and time permit.

Describe the Core Identifying Information

Certain core information is an essential part of any descriptive work. The extent and detail provided may vary depending on the content, context, and research uses of a body of records. Subsequent sections of this manual suggest a range of possible information to provide potential researchers to support and facilitate their interests. A few elements of information must be provided to achieve the goal of access. Because these elements are so essential to description, and ultimately to the retrieval of archival records, considerable professional discussion has taken place regarding the nature of this information, how to create it in a clear and consistent manner, and what standards to use in presenting it in descriptive tools. *Describing Archives: A Content Standard* provides substantial direction in these areas, addressing a range of situations, choices, and decisions the archivist will need to make, and it should guide the specifics in developing content for each of the following areas. Basic practices and issues will be noted here, but DACS, or in Canada the *Rules for Archival Description,* Second Edition (RAD2), should be used for specifics of implementation. Each provides considerable detail on specific situations, complexities, and a variety of common complications an archivist may encounter.

In keeping with the principles of provenance and *respect des fonds,* the archivist should clearly identify the person or organization responsible for creating, accumulating, or maintaining the group of records being described. While this often sounds fairly simple, a range of issues can arise. At times, archivists are tempted to identify the name

---

Figure 4-12 Core Elements of Descriptive Information

- *name of the person or organization* responsible for creating, accumulating, or maintaining the group of records being described. Often referred to as the "creator" of the group of records.
- *title* of the group of records being described (and of subsequent subdivisions if they are so arranged)
- *dates* included in the records
- *quantity* of records being described

of a person who actually wrote many or all of the items in a group of records, particularly when that person is well known. However, it is not the creation of the individual items in a group of records, but the bringing together of those records for personal, organizational, or business reasons that determines the name to be associated with the actual group of records itself. If, after careful research into the records it is not possible to identify the person or organization responsible for creating, accumulating, or maintaining the records, no creator is named. (See examples in appendix E.)

The title for a group of records will be the first descriptive item a user is likely to look at, particularly in an on-line catalog. As a result, the more clearly it describes the forms of materials, subject, or nature of the records, the more helpful it will be. Clear, descriptive titles should be provided at each level described. For example, in an on-line catalog, the title "Katherine Valdez Synchronized Swimming Collection" gives the user an immediate understanding of the subject focus, as opposed to the generality of "Katherine Valdez Collection."

The most basic dates to include in a core description are those indicating the span of time covered by the records, commonly referred to as the "inclusive dates." This would indicate the earliest date and latest date for which records exist in the group or series of records. Other types of dates may also be important to understanding the records, such as dates of records-keeping activity, dates relating to the person or organization, or the dates of records from a particular period of time (i.e., bulk dates or predominant dates). These are addressed in later sections of this manual; inclusive dates are the absolute minimum essential type to include in any description.

The final core element of information to include in a description is physical quantity. It is essential for both staff and users to know the extent of the records. Archivists commonly record this as cubic or linear feet to make the quantity clear. It is usually not helpful to a user to describe records solely in terms of volumes or "boxes," which may vary wildly in size from tiny to oversize, or in number of items, which is difficult to comprehend.

Figure 4-13 Core Description of Sample Records

Personal records:
　Charles E. Williams Papers, 1909–1930
　3 linear feet

Organizational records:
　Hot Coffee, Nevada, Town Clerk
　Town Board Meeting Minutes, 1981–1995
　10 cubic feet

Collection:
　Katherine Valdez Synchronized Swimming Collection, 1930–1995
　8 cubic feet

Describe the Contextual Information

Context, as previously noted, is one of the most critical factors distinguishing archival description. It is essential to provide information on the context in which the records were created, assembled, or maintained to understand the records themselves, whether created by an organization or an individual. Because archival records are the "results" of a person or organization going about daily life or business, there are many unstated assumptions and conditions—these are the contextual clues that make it possible for researchers/users to understand the content of the records.

From the background research done before arrangement and description begin, a summary of the contextual information should be prepared to make available to users. Many archivists, particularly in manuscripts repositories, include this information as part of a larger finding aid. Archivists working with organizational records, where many series may relate to the same creating entity, are increasingly creating separate "administrative history" records that provide contextual information to which individual series descriptions may be linked. Contextual information and administrative or biographical histories are sometimes referred to in archival literature as "authority information," although that term can cause confusion for librarians for whom it has a related, but somewhat different use.[46]

Work has been underway for a number of years to codify and clarify the type of archival contextual information that should be included in archival access tools. The International Council on Archives' Ad Hoc Commission on Descriptive Standards developed the *International Standard Archival Authority Record for Corporate Bodies, Persons and Families* in 1996 to provide an initial set of data elements for this type of information.[47] Additional work is in progress to develop an XML document type definition for Encoded Archival Context information.[48] Both efforts recognize the need to standardize and place more attention on the contextual information that is essential to the archival process.

Figure 4-14 Contextual Information for Sample Records

(Contextual information for all three sample records is provided as part of the finding aids in appendix D.)

Charles E. Williams Papers, 1909–1930
3 linear feet

Biographical history:
Charles Edward Williams was born in Coatesville, Pennsylvania, in 1900 to Willa Jackson Williams and Martin James Williams. Charles was educated in the Coatesville Public Schools, then attended Cheyney State Teachers College (now Cheyney University), receiving his B.A. in teaching in 1921. He taught in the Baltimore City schools for seven years. He then attended Howard University, receiving his J.D. in 1930. During his teaching career, Charles met and married Evelyn Jane Johnson in 1923. They had three daughters, Mary Louise (born 1925), Helen Ann (born 1926, died 1930), and Emily Jane (born 1929).

(continued)

---

46 Librarians use authority records for headings management, that is, to manage the "authoritative" version of a heading. This ensures collocation in a library catalog. For a useful explanation of this concept as it relates to libraries and archives, see Cynthia J. Durance, "Authority Control: Beyond a Bowl of Alphabet Soup," *Archivaria* 35 (Spring 1993): 64–70.

47 International Council, ISAAR(CPF).

48 EAC Web site available at http://www.library.yale.edu.eac.

Figure 4-14 continued

He had one older brother, George James Williams (1897–1917). George enlisted in the New York 15th Regiment of the New York Guard (the Harlem Hellfighters) which was reconstituted as the 369th U.S. Infantry during World War I. George and Charles corresponded regularly through the war until George's death as the result of a mustard gas attack.

After graduating from Howard, Charles joined two classmates, Errol Peck and James Wilson in establishing the law firm of Peck, Williams and Wilson in Harlem. Williams focused in particular on legal services to African American musicians and artists. The firm was highly successful, eventually employing a staff of over 35 lawyers serving the Harlem community.

Williams retired in 1968 and continued to do pro bono work for Legal Aid in Harlem. He died of heart failure in 1972.

Figure 4-15 Common Types of Contextual Information to Provide

- *Name(s)* the person/family/organization was known by, variant names, pseudonyms
- *Function, activity, or role* for which the records were created, used, and assembled
- *Enabling legislation, regulations, or governing documents* that define an organization's mission and sphere of activity
- *Significant accomplishments* that are reflected in the records or that might affect the content of the records
- *Personal or professional perspectives* that might affect understanding of the records
- *Date(s) of existence,* important dates in the life of the person/organization
- *Date(s) of records-keeping activity* when they differ from the inclusive or bulk dates of the records themselves
- *Historical period* in which the records were created
- *Place or geographical area* where the person(s) lived or the organization operated
- *Relationships* with other organizations, persons, families

Describe Physical Characteristics

Description of physical characteristics is essential information for both the user and the archivist. Information on extent will provide clues to a researcher as to the amount of time and effort that may be necessary to review a body of records. With electronic records, it may inform the potential user of the equipment that will be necessary to effectively access and understand the records. Both archivist and user should be aware of any physical conditions that may restrict or make access difficult (such as severe burn damage).

Common types of physical descriptive information to provide

- *Quantity/extent of the records* gives users an idea of how much material they may need to look at, and staff a sense of how much they will need to retrieve. In addition to the core information described above, more detail may be helpful for users. Precise terms should be used so the number and type of containers are clear. While no specific standards for recording this information exist, each repository should develop a consistent method for identifying quantity/extent and faithfully implement the agreed-upon approach.

- *Size of the records when not on standard paper* provides further information both for users and for staff responsible for retrieval and storage.

- *Additional formats* lets users know if the original exists in other forms that may be easier to use.

- *Bulk dates* indicate the time period covered by the majority of the records when the inclusive dates do not, or identify gaps.

- *Organization and arrangement of the records* provides users with an understanding of the physical groups in which the records exist and whether an internal system exists for ordering the records (such as alphabetical, numerical). Such information will be useful in planning research time.

Figure 4-16 Physical Information for Sample Records

Hot Coffee, Nevada, Town Clerk.
Election Records, 1920–1995
8 cubic feet (consisting of 20 bound volumes)
Organized chronologically

Charles E. Williams Papers, 1909–1930
3 linear feet including 25 photographs

Describe the Informational Contents

Archival description addresses description of content in particularly unique ways. Because archival records are generally the product of activity, the content can and most often will reflect a wide range of information. Archivists face the challenge of providing a description of informational content that summarizes the extent and variety of people, subjects, places, events, and issues reflected in a group of records.

Identifying all content precisely is probably impossible. Within even one letter in the personal papers of an individual, an amazing range of topics may be covered. Given the increasing volume of modern manuscript and archival records, it would be an insurmountable task to conduct any deep subject analysis. More significantly, that level of analysis would likely be unproductive for users, since their search approaches may vary considerably based on the purpose of their research. For example, for a group of land records including deeds and maps, genealogists would prefer a listing of all individual names, while social historians might like information on types of groups represented, and a land surveyor would want detailed access to geophysical information.

In addition, specific subject analysis based on anticipated researcher uses can be constrained by contemporary directions in research. Recently, historians working on the topic of anorexia nervosa have found diaries, medical records, and other information relevant to this topic as early as 1870. None of the archival finding aids provided the medical term for this disease, although the professional medical literature of that time uses the terminology. While the term was in active use throughout the period when records were described, the issue was not perceived as an important general topic worth noting in a finding aid.[49]

Facing all those challenges, archival content description can provide essentially a "blunt pointer" to direct users to some reasonable body of records for a closer look through the lens of their particular research need or focus. Informational content can provide a concise synopsis that potential researchers can use to decide whether relevant information is likely to be available, allowing them to decide whether to search the records further or not. For users with more precise name, place, event, or topical needs, searching container/folder lists can provide some ability to hone in on more specific, relevant components. With the increasing availability of automated access to detailed finding aids,[50] archivists are more readily able to provide users with the capacity to conduct both broad informational searches and some specific searches as well within the range of standard archival finding aids.

Common types of informational content to provide

- *Types of materials/formats* regularly found in the records

- *Names of people and organizations* predominant in the records

- *Names of prominent people* who either created information contained in or who are discussed in the records

- *Subject matter, common themes, and focuses* found in the records

- *Events* noted in the records or to which the records relate

- *Geographic locations* that are important in the records

- *Time period* to which the records relate if of significance to understand the records

---

49 E-mail to author from Joan Jacobs Brumberg, professor of history, Cornell University, May 2002.

50 See the next section in this chapter for information on automated approaches to access.

Figure 4-17 Informational Content for Sample Records

Contents Summary:
The papers consist of school report cards, essays, artwork, photographs, and reports from Williams's elementary, secondary, and college education. Correspondence is also included between Charles and his brother, George Williams, during World War I when George served in the 369th U.S. Infantry in Europe.

Series I: School and college records, 1907–1930
The papers contain records from Williams's years at Fourth Street Elementary School, Coatesville Junior and Senior High School, Cheyney State College, and Howard University.

Elementary school records include report cards for first through sixth grade. They provide letter grades for the various subjects taught. For grades three through six, the report cards also have narrative comments on Williams's performance in school.

Junior and senior high records include report cards for each grade except ninth. The report cards provide letter grades and narrative comments only for twelfth grade. Six essays written by Williams for his high school American history course are also included. They focus on the history of African American music and art in the U.S., as well as on Jim Crow policies after the Civil War. They provide insight into Williams's perspectives on the need to include African Americans in the written history of the United States.

College transcripts are included for Williams's matriculation at Cheyney State College where he majored in history education and received a B.A. Essays and reports focus on a range of topics in history from biographical essays on African American leaders to musical forms such as minstrel shows, jazz, and gospel music. Photographs of Williams, his fiancée, and his parents visiting Cheyney are included.

(continued)

Figure 4-17 continued

College transcripts relate to Williams's degree in jurisprudence at Howard University. Photographs of Williams's graduation are included.

Series II: World War I letters to and from George Williams, 1916–1917
This series contains both carbon copies of Charles Williams's letters to his brother, George, as well as letters from George to Charles relating to George's service with the 369th U.S. Infantry. The letters provide particularly important information and personal perspectives on the prejudice George experienced during training in Spartanburg, South Carolina. There is also considerable information on George's experiences when the unit fought with the 16th Division of the French Army. Letters from Charles provide stories of his experiences in school and include information on family activities. The final letter in the series is the telegram advising the Williams family of George's death.

Provide Access Points/Index Terms

Unlike library catalog records, for which access points are a standard component, archival finding aids vary in providing an index or set of terms to assist users in locating information. Manuscripts collections, with a stronger tie to library practice, more often provide this additional route for researchers, while governmental archives perceive provenance information as the method by which researchers are more likely to gain access. An important study conducted by Richard Lytle in the 1980s shows that archives users favor neither approach, so making both available is necessary to support reference searches.[51]

Carefully selected access points are essential for users.

---

51 Richard H. Lytle, "Intellectual Access to Archives: II. Report of an Experiment Comparing Provenance and Content Indexing Methods of Subject Retrieval," *American Archivist* 43 (Spring 1980): 191–207.

Figure 4-18 Common Access Points and Index Terms

- *Name of creator,* or the name of the person or organization creating, accumulating, or maintaining the records, including variations of that name
- *Added entries,* or the additional person(s) or organizations responsible for creating, accumulating, or maintaining the records
- *Personal name(s)* of individuals who are subjects of the records
- *Corporate name(s)* of organizations that are subjects of the records
- *Topical term(s)* providing information on significant subjects
- *Geographic term(s)* identifying place names or physical features
- *Genre/form term(s)* providing information on the types of records or the style and technique of their intellectual content that are found within the larger group of records
- *Occupation term(s)* relating to jobs, avocations, or similar roles that are subjects of the records (but not the occupation of the records creator unless that is substantially reflected in the records)
- *Function term(s)* reflecting the activity or function that generated the records being described

The introduction of automated approaches focused further attention on the need to provide access points to archival finding aids, particularly on-line catalog records. When the MARC AMC Format included specific fields for common archival index terms, considerable, sometimes volatile, discussion ensued about both the nature and extent of access points, as well as the use of standardized thesauri and vocabulary lists. With the development of descriptive practice over the past decade, archivists have become fairly regular providers of access points and index terms both in on-line catalogs and in finding aids.

The specific techniques for subject analysis, selection of terminology, and use of controlled vocabularies are beyond the scope of this manual. Nonetheless, providing access points for finding aids and metadata for Web sites is crucial to ensure that researchers can first locate the archivist's carefully crafted descriptive finding aids and then find the relevant information within them.[52]

---

52 A number of articles, manuals, and training opportunities are available addressing the development of access points and subject indexing. See the bibliography for articles and manuals, and the SAA Web site for training sessions.

Figure 4-19 Indexing Terms for Sample Record

Hot Coffee, Nevada, Town Clerk
Election Records, 1920–1995
8 cubic feet (consisting of 20 bound volumes)
organized chronologically

Summary: The election records provide a list of registered voters for each year; a summary providing the total number of votes received by each candidate for each town office; and the signed oaths of office for each elected official. Records for the 1938 list of registered voters contain the names of over 100 voters who had not been in the previous year's registration list and for which fictitious addresses were supplied. Handwriting specialists from the State Police also determined that the signatures were all probably written by the same person.

Index terms:

Subjects:	Forms:
Elections—Nevada—Hot Coffee	Oaths
Functions:	Election returns
Registering voters	Voting registers
Monitoring elections	

Describe the Administrative Information Needed to Support Use

Information on how a body of records has been or needs to be managed will affect both user and archivist. Such information might include whether restrictions on access and use are imposed either by law or by donor request. Similarly, information on the "chain of custody" of a body of records may be significant—the content of records may be altered or compromised if the records of an individual were weeded by a family member before they were donated to an archives, or if the records of a government organization were out of the custody of that organization before being transferred to an archives. Information on actions that have been taken with records can be helpful in various circumstances to either the user or the archivist. This might include such information as whether records have been reformatted (into microfilm or digital images), whether and what kind of preservation treatments have been applied, or if records have been rearranged or weeded by the archives staff.

COMMON TYPES OF ADMINISTRATIVE INFORMATION

- *"Conditions governing access"* identify restrictions on access due to the records' physical condition, the records not being processed, or the records being stored off-site. They may also be restricted because of privacy law or donor-imposed restrictions.

- *"Conditions governing use"* identify conditions that may restrict use due to copyright or other legal agreements that require special permission to quote from, reproduce, or otherwise use the records.

- *"Other physical forms available"* lets users know that records may have been reformatted, digitized, or reproduced and which form may be preferable to use instead of the original.

- *"Custodial history/provenance"* highlights significant or unusual events or actions that may have happened to or with the records that could affect or alter their nature and contents, such as weeding by the family or being maintained out of the custody of the records creator before being placed in an archives.

- *"Actions taken on the records,"* such as preservation treatments, microfilming, reorganizing, or weeding by staff, can be useful information, particularly if they may have changed the extent or structure of the records.

Figure 4-20 Administrative Information for Sample Record

Hot Coffee, Nevada, Town Clerk
Registration of Births and Deaths, 1891–1975
5 cubic feet

Restrictions note: Access to records less than 75 years old are restricted under Nevada Laws of 1985 chapter 700. See the town clerk for information on access conditions for restricted records.

Additional physical formats available: Records were microfilmed in 1977. Users must use microfilm version.

Developing Access Tools

Archivists have historically developed a range of tools in an effort to make information about archival records available and useful for potential researchers. The structure, nature, and format of such tools have varied over time, and sometimes great controversy has raged over what term to call an access tool—but the ultimate purpose remains the same. The generic term for such access tools, *finding aid,* is defined as a "representation of, and/or a means of access to, archival material made or received by a repository in the course of establishing administrative or intellectual control over the archival material."[53] A range of finding aid types may be appropriate, but certain essential tools should be created to manage access to archival records. At a minimum, a basic finding aid (referred to by many archivists as an "inventory" or "descriptive inventory") should be developed for archival holdings. From that finding aid, additional finding aids can be created depending on the intended audience, the nature of the records, or the institutional goals.

Create a Finding Aid to the Records

Full finding aids for the three sample groups of records used for illustration in this manual are in appendix D.

As soon as archival records arrive in a repository, some very basic physical and intellectual control information should be provided. This is generally done through an accession form, the first, and most basic finding aid. (See figure 4-5.)

The core archival finding aid is the inventory.[54] Traditionally, archives and manuscripts repositories have developed this in paper form, but increasingly they are also making it available electronically. The finding aid, as pointed out in Steven L. Hensen's *Archives, Personal Papers, and Manuscripts,* Second Edition, then becomes the "chief source of information" for subsequent catalog records or other access tools developed to promote awareness or use of the records.

---

53 Society of American Archivists, *Describing Archives: A Content Standard.*

54 Some repositories use different terminology for this type of tool, variously calling it a register, a descriptive inventory, or simply a finding aid.

TYPICAL CONTENTS OF AN INVENTORY

- *Title page,* providing the proper name for a group of records, person or office responsible for creating the finding aid, name of the archival repository, and date the finding aid was created

- *Administrative or biographical history,* providing a summary narrative of contextual information needed to understand and interpret the records

- *Description of the records,* providing a succinct explanation of their informational contents and physical characteristics. Based on decisions made by the archivist regarding level of description, information may be provided for the overall group of records and may also include series, subseries, or even more detailed levels.

- *Administrative information* necessary to use the records, such as physical condition, additional forms available, and restrictions on access or use

- *Container/folder lists,* providing more detailed access to records that may be relevant to the user's research

- *Additional information,* to support the researcher's use of the records, such as a glossary of terms, a bibliography, a time line of important events, or similar explanatory information. For institutional records, organizational charts, lists of officials, or major functions might be included. For personal or family papers, a family tree, list of family member names, or places of residence and time period might be provided.

- *Indexes,* to assist the user in locating information within the inventory/finding aid, including personal, organizational or place names, events, major types of records, and major subjects

While inventories/finding aids have traditionally been provided in paper form, archives and manuscripts collections are increasingly furnishing on-line access to these tools using Encoded Archival Description (EAD), Hypertext Markup Language (HTML), Dynamic

Hypertext Markup Language (DHTML), or Extensible Markup Language (XML). These protocols allow inventories to be made available on-line with sufficient flexibility to accommodate a variety of institutional styles or the needs of particular groups of records.

Develop Additional Access Tools

Other types of access tools may be developed to support an institution's access and retrieval system and meet the needs of particular user groups. The inventory/finding aid can be used as the source for a range of other access tools. Each archival institution needs to assess the information needs and information-seeking behavior of both its staff and its constituents to determine what access tools are most productive and appropriate. Even with the availability of on-line access, staff members remain frequent "surrogates" in seeking information for users who call, write, e-mail, or arrive for on-site research. Users come to archival repositories (either literally or virtually) seeking information, and, as Richard Smiraglia notes, must convert their need into a set of questions or search strategies that will allow them to find information within the access tools provided.[55] Supporting the searching needs of both groups should be taken into consideration in developing access tools.

Jim Burke enters information into the Florida Bureau of Archives and Records Management database. Databases, whether off the shelf or created specifically for the collection, help the archives maintain control over collections. PHOTOGRAPH COURTESY FLORIDA BUREAU OF ARCHIVES AND RECORDS MANAGEMENT.

---

55 Richard Smiraglia, ed., *The Use of the MARC AMC Format* (New York: Haworth Press, 1990), 7.

Beyond the core inventory/finding aid, a number of additional access tools may be developed. These include:

CATALOGS. Card catalogs are traditionally a tool used predominantly by manuscripts repositories to provide subject and name access to inventories and records. This reflects the library traditions to which many manuscripts repositories are related. With the introduction of automation and the implementation of the MARC Format with archives and manuscripts, the vast majority of repositories with automated capabilities have developed on-line catalogs. Some have integrated their on-line catalogs into, or maintain them as a part of, a larger library catalog. Others have developed independent on-line catalogs on either microcomputer-based systems or mainframe systems. Catalog records, whether in card format or on-line, should provide summary information extracted from the fuller inventory or finding aid to provide users with a "blunt pointer" that allows them to decide whether it will be useful to consult the inventory or the archival repository for further information on the records.

Some archival repositories are collaborating on their on-line catalogs to provide broader access to holdings. These cooperative catalogs provide researchers the ability to search one catalog and find holdings on related topics, events, or people from a variety of institutions. The *National Union Catalog of Manuscript Collections (NUCMC)* was initially compiled by the Library of Congress as a "union catalog" for manuscripts in the United States and was published in volume form beginning in 1959.[56] Since 1986–87, NUCMC records have been created electronically in the Research Libraries Information Network (RLIN). RLIN is a bibliographic network created and maintained by the Research Libraries Group (RLG), a member-supported organization. Some 160 members in the United States, Canada, and internationally have now created over 700,000 bibliographic (or catalog) records relating to their archival and manuscript holdings.[57] The Online Computer Library Center (OCLC), also a membership organization of libraries and archives, supports WorldCat, a bibliographic network of over 300,000 archives/manuscripts bibliographic records, which also provides searching infor-

---

56 *NUCMC* Web site available at http://lcweb.loc.gov/coll/nucmc/.
57 RLG Web site available at http://www.rlg.org.

mation from its member institutions.[58] The Canadian Archival Information Network (CAIN), a national database developed with support from the Canadian Council of Archives, the National Archives of Canada, and the Department of Canadian Heritage, furnishes access to the holdings of most of the archival institutions across Canada.[59]

Some states and regions have developed collaborative catalog/bibliographic databases to provide access to archival records through summary on-line "catalog" records. The Colorado Alliance of Research Libraries (CARL) includes manuscripts and archival records in its "Prospector," a combined catalog from its sixteen members.[60] The New York State Archives provides access to summary catalog descriptions of holdings from over 1,500 historical records organizations in that state in its "Historic Documents Inventory" (HDI).[61]

In the *National Inventory of Documentary Sources,* the Chadwick-Healey Company undertook an initial effort at providing a "union catalog" of actual finding aids in the United States. Finding aids from archives and manuscripts repositories around the country were microfilmed and made available through an index. Currently, this tool is available on CD-ROM and on-line as part of the company's Web site, ArchivesUSA.[62]

Some recent collaborative efforts focus on developing cooperative Web sites for encoded finding aids, which generally provide users with deeper levels of access. The *Online Archive of California,* for example, which developed from the Berkeley Finding Aid Project, furnishes a searchable database of collection descriptions linked to finding aids as well as to digital facsimiles of archives and manuscripts records. This project also served as the test-bed for the development of Encoded Archival Description (EAD) for finding aids. Other collaborative efforts are using this model to create collective access to finding aids based on regions or topics.[63]

---

58 OCLC Web site available at http://www.oclc.org/home.

59 CAIN Web site available at http://www.archivescanada.ca/.

60 Prospector on-line catalog available at http://prospector.coalliance.org/.

61 HDI on-line catalog available at http://www.nysed.gov.

62 ArchivesUSA also includes a directory of archival and manuscripts repositories in the U.S. and the Library of Congress's *National Union Catalog of Manuscripts Collections.* Web site available at http://www.archives.chadwyck.com/.

63 See, for example, North Carolina ECHO Project available on-line at http://www.ncecho.org/ncead or the *Guide to Australian Literary Manuscripts* available on-line at http://findaid.library.uwa.edu.au/.

GUIDES. Until the introduction of automation, archives and manuscripts repositories generally considered a summary guide to their holdings as the best way to provide general access to the whole collection. A summary guide furnishes overview information on the records held, enabling the user to determine whether it might be worthwhile to contact the repository for further information from finding aids. While on-line catalogs and Web sites have assumed much of this "blunt pointer" function, some institutions still find a summary guide useful for users unfamiliar with computer access, or as a public relations tool for introducing the archives to potential supporters and users.

In addition to summary guides, topical guides to particular areas of research are frequently developed both on-line and in published form. Such guides can be useful to bring together information from areas of high research interest and to enable the archives to include information beyond the description of specific records.

INDEXES. Despite the archival imperative to describe records first at the general level, some records require more detailed access to best serve user needs. Developing such tools should reflect real need for a substantial base of users, not simply for the loudest few, or for the archivist's personal interest. The time and effort to develop indexes, whether manual or automated, should be warranted by the demand and use. Such tools are often important for records containing individual documents, such as literary manuscripts, photographs, maps, and genealogical information, that are used repeatedly.

CALENDARS. Nineteenth- and early twentieth-century descriptive practices often focused on the creation of calendars to records. A calendar involves incredibly labor-intensive work and generally consists of providing item-level information on a group of records such as date, description of the item, description of contents, and other consistent information. Calendaring is generally now reserved for the most important records of unusual intrinsic or informational value. Calendaring does not replace description at the general level, but should be undertaken after the broader descriptive finding aid has been developed.

OTHER ACCESS TOOLS. The introduction of the Internet as a tool for making descriptive information available in new ways has challenged archivists to create new access tools. In addition to making or adapting traditional finding aids for presentation on the Web, other approaches to providing information on archival holdings are being pursued.

"Pathfinders" provide a useful automated method for facilitating user access to records. Some archives identify major holdings on a popular search topic and explain how to use the relevant series, as in the *Pathfinder for Women's History in the National Archives,*[64] which provides essentially a more facile, flexible approach on the order of a special subject guide. Pathfinders can also be developed to provide more detailed information on the intricacies of searching for specific types of records, as ably demonstrated in the Archives of Ontario's pathfinders for *Finding a Birth Registration; Finding a Marriage Registration;* and *Finding a Death Registration.*[65]

The rapidly increasing availability of digital images offers users the opportunity to make copies of actual records available as part of an archives' overall access system. The expectations among researchers and the general public for the availability of such images are high, and many archival institutions are responding quickly to the demands. Digital collections may come from one manuscripts group or archival series or from selected holdings on a topic from one repository, or they may

---

64 The *Pathfinder for Women's History in the National Archives* is available at http://www.archives.gov/research_room/alic/bibliographies/women.html.
65 The pathfinders for *Finding a Birth Registration; Finding a Marriage Registration;* and *Finding a Death Registration* are available at http://archives.gov.on.ca/english/ interloan/vsmain.htm.

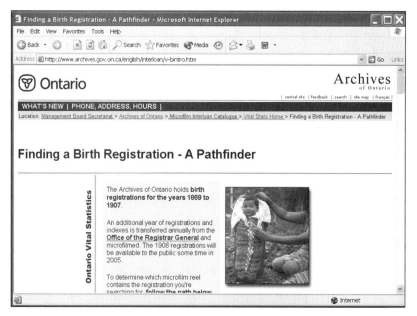

This pathfinder was developed by the Archives of Ontario to provide assistance to geneological patrons.

Figure 4-21 Examples of Digital Collections

- The American Memory project hosted by the Library of Congress (http://memory.loc.gov/ammem/) is the largest digital collection in the u.s. It has over 60 separate collections on a wide variety of subjects.
- The Colorado Digitization Project (http://coloradodigital. coalliance.org/) is a collaborative effort of over 26 archives, historical societies, libraries, and museums to provide digital images of archival and manuscript resources around the state.
- The Emilio Segré Visual Archives (http://www.aip.org/history/ esva/) is a collection of some 25,000 visual materials from the Niels Bohr Library of the Center for History of Physics at the American Institute of Physics. The collection focuses primarily on American physicists and astronomers of the twentieth century.
- The Images of African Americans from the 19th Century (http:// digital.nypl.org/schomburg/images_aa19/main.html), created by the Schomburg Center for Research in Black Culture, New York Public Library, provides a virtual collection of digitized images from the center's holdings.

involve collaborative efforts to digitize records from a group of repositories on a theme. Such collections pose several challenges for archival description. In some systems, such as the *Online Archive of California,* access to the digital images is integrated into the hierarchy of finding aids. In other cases, access to digital images is managed separately, and archivists need to determine the extent and type of descriptive information to make available on each image. No common approach has developed as of this writing for the metadata used with digital images, but a number of digital imaging projects use Dublin Core metadata as the guide for data elements to include.[66]

Archivists increasingly face the need to carefully plan a rational system for access to their holdings. Until only recently, a combined paper-based approach, including inventories, summary guides, and perhaps special indexes or topical guides, was the staple of archival access. The opportunities offered by automation through on-line catalogs, databases, search tools, and Web-based technology have vastly expanded the options for access. Archivists face many challenges in balancing the advantages of standard and predictable access tools to facilitate user access with the potential for facile new approaches to access in the coming decade.

Professional Standards for Archival Arrangement and Description

Over the past two decades, archivists in the United States and Canada have become increasingly involved in the development and implementation of standards for arrangement and description both nationally and internationally. The language surrounding standards can be complex and sometimes daunting. For the purposes of understanding standards in the context of archival description, it is first useful to define some essential terminology. Technical standards are defined as "an explicit definition that can be communicated, which is not subject to unilateral change without notice and which, if properly followed,

---

66 Information on the Dublin Core Metadata Initiative is available at http://dublincore.org/. An example of how Dublin Core has been implemented is the Colorado Digitization Project's background information at http://coloradodigital.coalliance.org/standard.html.

will yield consistent results."[67] While archivists may use such standards such as z39.50 for searching in their on-line catalogs, for example, technical standards are not developed for the archival community. Instead, archivists generally have developed conventions (also known as "rules" or "professional standards") that have been approved by a relevant professional organization such as the Society of American Archivists, the Canadian Council on Archives, or the International Council on Archives.[68] Some archival practices are guidelines, that is, recommendations or commonly shared approaches that can lead to better quality descriptive practice. Guidelines provide "best practices" against which repositories can measure themselves, or can implement locally. Guidelines do not have the distinction of receiving formal professional review and approval, however, which professional standards have.

Professional standards, or conventions for archival description, are important in three areas, and considerable effort has been invested over the past two decades in their development and adoption.

Archival Data Structure Standards

Data structure standards define what data elements of information are contained in the components of or are allowable in an information system. The following data structure standards are currently in use. (See bibliography for information on on-line and hard copy availability.)

- MARC 21 (also known by its earlier name, MARC Format for Bibliographic Data). Originally created as a separate format for archives and manuscripts (MARC AMC), the separate MARC formats were integrated into one single data structure standard. U.S. and Canadian MARC were subsequently merged into MARC 21. MARC was adopted officially by the Society of American Archivists as an archival professional standard.

---

67 Walt Crawford, *Technical Standards: An Introduction for Librarians* (White Plains, N.Y.: Knowledge Industry Publications, 1986): 6–7.

68 For an instructive explanation of standards, see "Archival Descriptive Standards: Establishing a Process for Their Development and Implementation. Report of the Working Group on Standards for Archival Description," *American Archivist* 52 (Fall 1989): 440–77.

- Encoded Archival Description (EAD). EAD provides a document type definition (DTD) for encoding archival finding aids using XML (Extensible Markup Language). The Society of American Archivists has adopted EAD officially. It is also being used in a number of other countries.

- General International Standard Archival Description. ISAD(G) was created by the Ad Hoc Commission on Descriptive Standards as part of the work of the International Council on Archives (ICA). It incorporates data content information along with data structure. The ICA and a number of individual countries have officially adopted it.

Archival Data Content Standards

Data content standards provide rules for entering the information in an archival description. These rules furnish consistent ways to record information such as punctuation, formats for dates and quantities, and required vs. optional items. The consistency provided by data content standards supports the user's understanding of the information about the records and also facilitates retrieval. The following data content standards are currently in use. (See bibliography for information on on-line and hard copy availability.)

- *Describing Archives: A Content Standard* was in publication production at the time this manual was written. It replaces *Archives, Personal Papers, and Manuscripts,* Second Edition. Both volumes provide the archival community with a companion to the *Anglo-American Cataloguing Rules 2.*

- *Rules for Archival Description,* Second Edition was in publication production at the time this manual was written. It revises and updates the original *Rules for Archival Description* which was developed by the Canadian archival community.

Content standards for specific forms of material have also been developed, including

- *Graphic Materials: Rules for Describing Original Items and Historical Collections (GIHC)*

- *Archival Moving Image Materials: A Cataloging Manual (AMIM)*

- *Oral History Cataloging Manual (OHCM)*

Archival Data Value Standards

Data value standards provide actual lists of words, terms, or codes to use for specific data elements, again providing consistency for users and facilitating retrieval. A range of thesauri and vocabulary lists are commonly used in archives. The selection of vocabularies or lists will depend to some extent on the repository, its mission, and its research constituency. Generally, repositories try to avoid developing vocabulary lists that apply only to their own holdings. Users are more successful in their searches on-line when a predictable vocabulary is used, and maintenance of thesauri and lists is very labor intensive. Some very specialized archives do find it useful to create their own lists, but they make use of the more common standardized thesauri and lists as well.

Figure 4-22 Examples of Data Value Thesauri and Vocabulary Lists

See bibliography for information on on-line and hard copy availability.

- *Library of Congress Subject Headings*
- *Art and Architecture Thesaurus*
- *Library of Congress Thesaurus for Graphic Materials: Topical Terms for Subject Access*
- *Genre Terms: A Thesaurus for Use in Rare Book and Special Collections Cataloguing*
- *Descriptive Terms for Graphic Materials: Genre and Physical Characteristic Headings*
- *Moving Image Materials: Genre Terms*

Conclusion, Future Directions, and Issues

Archival descriptive practices enjoyed the luxury of being anachronistic and institution-specific for many years. The introduction of automated access and the Internet, however, accelerated demands and expectations for a higher quality, more consistent, and predictable approach to description. Since the early 1980s, the archival community has addressed that challenge with increasingly sophisticated approaches to arrangement, description, use of standards, controlled vocabularies, and data structure standards like MARC and EAD.

Arrangement and description are critical components of the archival process. Done well, they can ensure an accurate and useful representation of records for use by a wide range of users. In order to do arrangement and description well, however, archivists need to balance a range of technical, historical, and professional skills. Given the dynamic nature of professional standards for archival description, archivists involved in this function need to make a conscious effort to maintain an awareness of current work nationally and internationally in this area.

The archival community still faces challenges in developing consistent and useful practices for description of electronic records, for digital images, and for those records that are "born digital." The practice of archival arrangement and description remains largely based on paper records. The principles of provenance and original order can still have relevance with these types of records, but practices and finding tools need to reflect at least intelligent adaptation if not whole new approaches. It may well be that solving the challenges of newer formats of records will inspire the archival profession to create new tools that will in fact be more facile and useful for researchers and can be used for traditional records as well.

Archivists involved in description also need to undertake their work in constant collaboration with other archivists and with related professional groups. Working closely with records managers and appraisal staff will ensure that timely and useful information is transferred to support and speed the process of arrangement and description. Interaction with reference and public programming staff will ensure that finding aids and access systems better address user needs and interests.

In addition to developments in the archival profession, description archivists need to maintain an awareness of the types of researchers who can and who are using their archival holdings. Understanding the search strategies they employ, the methods they use in their research, and the technical options they can and are willing to use is essential for the archivist who wishes to provide an effective access system. While maintaining compliance with professional standards, the archivist can develop finding aids and other descriptive tools to support the capacity of the researcher to identify potential records for use.

This manual has provided a basic introduction to the core concepts, practices, and processes involved in archival arrangement and description. Additional training, reading, and practical application are imperative for the archivist to develop a deeper understanding of archival arrangement and description. The challenges for the archivist involved in description are many, but are well worth the effort to ensure the survival and availability of our cultural heritage.

Glossary

Sources for these definitions are as follows. Full bibliographic citations for these resources are in the bibliography.

Describing Archives: A Content Standard (2004) [DACS]

A Glossary for Archivists, Manuscripts Curators, and Records Managers (1992) [GAMCRM]

A Glossary of Archival and Records Terminology (2005) [GART]

ISAD(G): General International Standard Archival Description, 2nd ed. (2000) *[ISAD(G)]*

Accession: 1. Materials physically and legally transferred to a repository as a unit at a single time; 2. To take legal and physical custody of a group of records or other materials and to formally document their receipt. *[GART]*

Accrual (accretion): Materials added to an existing body of records or papers; an accretion. *[DACS]*

Archives: The documents created or received and accumulated by a person or organization in the course of the conduct of affairs and preserved because of their continuing value. Historically, the term referred more narrowly to the noncurrent records of an organization or institution preserved because of their continuing value. [GAMCRM]

Arrangement: The process of organizing materials with respect to their provenance and original order, to protect their context and to achieve physical and intellectual control over the materials. [DACS]

Collection: 1. A group of materials with some unifying characteristics; 2. Materials assembled by a person, organization, or repository from a variety of sources; 3. The holdings of a repository. [DACS]

Content: The information that a document is meant to convey. [GAMCRM]

Context: The organizational, functional, and operational circumstances surrounding materials' creation, receipt, storage, or use and its relationship to other materials. [GART]

Date(s) of recordkeeping activity: The date(s) during which the unit being described was created, accumulated, and maintained as an aggregation of records by the creator of the records. [DACS]

Description: The creation of an accurate representation of a unit of archival material by the process of capturing, collating, analyzing, and organizing information that serves to identify archival material and explain the context and record system(s) that produced it. [DACS]

Finding aid: A representation of, and/or a means of access to, archival materials made or received by a repository in the course of establishing administrative or intellectual control over the archival material. [DACS]

Fonds: The whole of the documents, regardless of form or medium, automatically and organically created and/or accumulated and used by a particular person, family, or corporate body in the course of the creator's activities and functions. *[ISAD(G)]*

Life cycle: The life span of a record from its creation or receipt to its final disposition. *[GAMCRM]*

Manuscripts: Documents of manuscript character usually having historical or literary value or significance. The term is variously used to refer to archives, to assembled collections, and to individual documents acquired by a manuscripts repository because of their significance. *[GAMCRM]*

Multilevel description: 1. The preparation of descriptions that are related to one another in a part-to-whole relationship and that need complete identification of both the parts and the comprehensive whole in multiple descriptive records; 2. A finding aid or other access tool that consists of separate, interrelated descriptions of the whole and its parts, reflecting the hierarchy of the materials being described. *[DACS]*

Original order: The principle that the order of the records that was established by the creator should be retained whenever possible to preserve existing relationships between the documents and the evidential value inherent in their order. See also *respect des fonds*. *[DACS]*

Phased preservation: A preservation management technique emphasizing actions that have the greatest impact on the preservation of collections as a whole rather than concentrating on individual items. *[GART]*

Provenance: The relationships between records and the organizations or individuals that created, assembled, accumulated, and/or maintained and used them in the conduct of personal or corporate activity. See also *respect des fonds*. *[DACS]*

Record group: A body of organizationally related records established on the basis of provenance by an archives for control purposes. A record group constitutes the archives (or the part thereof in the custody of an archival institution) of an autonomous recordkeeping corporate body. *[GAMCRM]*

Respect des fonds: The principle that the records created, accumulated, assembled, and/or maintained and used by an organization or individual must be kept together in their original order if it exists or has been maintained and not be mixed or combined with the records of another individual or corporate body. See also *original order, provenance. [DACS]*

Series: Documents arranged in accordance with a filing system or maintained as a unit because they result from the same accumulation or filing process, the same function, or the same activity; have a particular form or subject; or because of some other relationship arising out of their creation, receipt, or use. *[DACS]*

Bibliography

A wealth of resources on various aspects of archival arrangement and description are available. This bibliography is not intended to be comprehensive. Instead, it provides citations to a selection of resources that expand on topics and issues contained in this manual. The items include "classics" of archival literature as well as recent writings, which reflect a variety of opinions and approaches drawing predominantly on u.s. and Canadian practice.

Manuals and Guidelines for the Practice of Arrangement and Description

A number of manuals provide general guidance on arrangement and description with a range of intended audiences:

Carmicheal, David W. *Organizing Archival Records: A Practical Manual for Small Archives.* Walnut Creek, Calif.: AltaMira Press, 2003. Provides a clear, practical introduction for staff and volunteers in smaller repositories.

Ellis, Judith, ed. *Keeping Archives,* 2nd ed. Port Melbourne, Victoria, Australia: D. W. Thorpe/Australian Society of Archivists, 1993. In this general manual developed for the Australian archival community, the chapter on arrangement and description provides case studies and practical procedures. A 3rd edition of this title is due in 2005 by the National Archives of Australia.

Fox, Michael J. and Peter L. Wilkerson. *Introduction to Archival Organization and Description.* Los Angeles: Getty Information Institute, 1998. Aimed at a museum and cultural organization audience, this book provides a clear introduction to essential archival concepts and practices. It also provides a practical section, "An over-the-shoulder view of an archivist at work," which is available on-line at http://www.getty.edu/research/institute/standards/introarchives/.

Sample Forms for Archival and Records Management Programs. Chicago: Society of American Archivists and ARMA International, 2002.

Several manuals provide guidance in specific areas of arrangement and description or for specific formats and genres:

AMIM Revision Committee, Motion Picture, Broadcasting, and Recorded Sound Division. *Archival Moving Image Materials: A Cataloging Manual (AMIM).* Washington, D.C.: Library of Congress, 2000.

Betz, Elisabeth (Parker), comp. *Graphic Materials: Rules for Describing Original Items and Historical Collections.* Washington, D.C.: Library of Congress, 1982. On-line version available at http://www.loc.gov/rr/print/gm/graphmat.html.

Black, Elizabeth. *Authority Control: A Manual for Archivists.* Ottawa: Bureau of Canadian Archivists, 1991.

Bureau of Canadian Archivists. *Subject Indexing for Archivists. Report of the Subject Indexing Working Group, Planning Committee on Descriptive Standards.* Ottawa: Bureau of Canadian Archivists, 1992.

Matters, Marion, comp. *Oral History Cataloging Manual.* Chicago: Society of American Archivists, 1995.

Foundation/Classic Texts on Archival Description

Holmes, Oliver W. "Archival Arrangement—Five Different Operations at Five Different Levels." *American Archivist* 27 (January 1964): 21–41.

Muller, S., J. A. Feith, and R. Fruin. *Manual for the Arrangement and Description of Archives.* New York: H. W. Wilson Company, 1968. This classic manual, translated from the Dutch, continues to provide excellent information particularly for arrangement and description of government records.

Schellenberg, T. R. "Archival Principles of Arrangement." In *A Modern Archives Reader,* edited by Maygene Daniels and Timothy Walch, 149–61. Washington, D.C.: National Archives Trust Fund Board, 1984.

Core Concepts and Principles

Bearman, David. *Archival Methods.* Archives and Museum Informatics Technical Report 3, no. 1. Pittsburgh: Archives and Museum Informatics, 1989.

Bellardo, Lewis J. and Lynn Lady Bellardo, comps. *A Glossary for Archivists, Manuscript Curators, and Records Managers.* Chicago: Society of American Archivists, 1992.

Bureau of Canadian Archivists. *The Archival Fonds: From Theory to Practice.* Ottawa: Bureau of Canadian Archivists, 1992.

Fox, Michael J. "Descriptive Cataloging for Archival Materials." In *Describing Archival Materials: The Use of the MARC AMC Format,* edited by Richard P. Smiraglia, 17–34. New York: Haworth Press, 1990.

Pearce-Moses, Richard, comp. *A Glossary of Archival and Records Terminology.* Chicago: Society of American Archivists, 2005.

Issues and Special Topics in Arrangement and Description

Bearman, David. "'Who About What?' or 'From Whence, Why and How?': Establishing Intellectual Control Standards to Provide for Access to Archival Materials." In *Archives, Automation, and Access,* edited by Peter Baskerville and Chad Gaffield, 39–47. Vancouver: University of British Columbia, 1986.

———. "Authority Control Issues and Prospects." *American Archivist* 52 (Summer 1989): 286–99.

———. *Towards National Information Systems for Archives and Manuscript Repositories: The National Information Systems Task Force (NISTF) Papers, 1981–1984.* Chicago: Society of American Archivists, 1987.

———— and Richard Szary. "Beyond Authorized Headings: Authorities as Reference Files in a Multi-Disciplinary Setting." In *Authority Control Symposium,* edited by Karen Muller, 69-78. Occasional Papers 6. Tucson, Ariz.: Art Libraries of North American, 1987.

Dooley, Jackie M. "Subject Indexing in Context." *American Archivist* 55 (Spring 1992): 344–54.

———— and Helena Zinkham. "The Object as 'Subject': Providing Access to Genre, Form of Material, and Physical Characteristics." In *Beyond the Book: Extending* MARC *for Subject Access,* edited by Toni Petersen and Pat Molholt, 60–65. Boston: G. K. Hall, 1990.

Durance, Cynthia J. "Authority Control: Beyond a Bowl of Alphabet Soup." *Archivaria* 35 (Spring 1993): 38–46.

"Encoded Archival Description: Special Issues 1 and 2." *American Archivist* 59 and 60 (Summer and Fall 1997). These two special issues provide a wealth of articles on the development of EAD, special application issues, and the affect of EAD on repository practice.

Evans, Max J. "Authority Control: An Alternative to the Record Group Concept." *American Archivist* 49 (Summer 1986): 249–61.

Krawczyk, Bob. "Cross Reference Heaven: The Abandonment of the Fonds as the Primary Level of Arrangement for Ontario Government Records." *Archivaria* 48 (Fall 1999): 131–53.

Lytle, Richard H. "Intellectual Access to Archives: I. Provenance and Content Indexing Methods of Subject Retrieval." *American Archivist* 43 (Winter 1980): 64–75.

————. "Intellectual Access to Archives: II. Report of an Experiment Comparing Provenance and Content Indexing Methods of Subject Retrieval." *American Archivist* 43 (Spring 1980): 191–207.

Michaelson, Avra. "Description and Reference in the Age of Automation." *American Archivist* 50 (Spring 1987): 192–208.

Pitti, Daniel V. and Wendy M. Duff, eds. *Encoded Archival Description on the Internet.* New York: Haworth Press, 2001. Includes a range of articles on the development and implementation of EAD in varying types of repositories, as consortial projects, and with museums.

Roe, Kathleen D. "Enhanced Authority Control: Is It Time?" *Archivaria* 35 (Spring 1993): 119–29.

Schellenberg, Theodore R. *The Management of Archives.* New York: Columbia University Press, 1965. Reprinted with a new introduction in 1981 by the National Archives and Records Administration.

Smiraglia, Richard, ed. *Describing Archival Materials: The Use of the* MARC AMC *Format.* New York: Haworth Press, 1990. This volume contains a range of articles explaining the structure and application of the MARC AMC format as well as its use with special formats.

Weber, Lisa B. "The 'Other' US MARC Formats: Authorities and Holdings. Do We Care to Be Partners in This Dance, Too?" *American Archivist* 53 (Winter 1990): 44–51.

Development of Descriptive Standards

Bureau of Canadian Archivists. *Toward Descriptive Standards: Report and Recommendations of the Canadian Working Group on Archival Descriptive Standards.* Ottawa: Bureau of Canadian Archivists, 1985.

Duff, Wendy M. and Kent M. Haworth. "The Reclamation of Archival Description: The Canadian Perspective." *Archivaria* 31 (Winter 1990–1991): 26–35.

———. "Advancing Archival Description: A Model for Rationalising North American Descriptive Standards." *Archives and Manuscripts* 25 (November 1997): 194–217.

Hensen, Steven L. "The First Shall be First: APPM and Its Impact on American Archival Description." *Archivaria* 35 (Spring 1993): 64–70.

Working Group on Standards for Archival Description. "Archival Description Standards: Establishing a Process for Their Development and Implementation." *American Archivist* 52 (Fall 1989): 430–502.

Standards and Guidelines

American Library Association. *Anglo-American Cataloguing Rules,* 2nd Edition. Chicago: ALA, 1988.

Art and Architecture Thesaurus. J. Paul Getty Trust, 2000. Available on-line at http://www.getty.edu/research/tools/vocabulary/aat/index.html.

Bureau of Canadian Archivists. *Rules for Archival Description.* Ottawa: Bureau of Canadian Archivists, 1990, rev. ed., 2001. *RAD2* forthcoming (see http://cdncouncilarchives.ca/archdesrules.html).

Hensen, Steven L. *Archives, Personal Papers, and Manuscripts.* 2nd ed. Chicago: Society of American Archivists, 1989.

International Council on Archives. *ISAD(G): General International Standard Archival Description.* 2nd ed. Ottawa: ICA, 2000.

———. *ISAAR(CPF): International Standard Archival Authority Record for Corporate Bodies, Persons and Families.* Ottawa: ICA, 1996.

Library of Congress. *MARC 21 Format for Bibliographic Data.* Washington D.C.: Library of Congress, 1999. Also available on-line at http://lcweb.loc.gov/cds/marcdoc.html#marc21.

———. *Moving Image Materials: Genre Terms.* Washington D.C.: Library of Congress, 1987. This publication is out of print. An updated version is available on-line at http://www.loc.gov/rr/mopic/migintro.html.

———. *Thesaurus for Graphic Materials: Topical Terms for Subject Access.* Washington D.C.: Library of Congress, 1995. This publication is out of print. An updated version is available on-line at http://www.loc.gov/rr/print/tgm1.

Society of American Archivists. *Describing Archives: A Content Standard.* Chicago: Society of American Archivists, 2004.

Walch, Victoria Irons. *Standards for Archival Description: A Handbook.* Chicago: Society of American Archivists, 1994. Available on-line at http://www.archivists.org/catalog/stds99/index.html. This on-line updated version of the printed publication describes technical standards, conventions, and guidelines used by archivists in describing holdings and repositories. It provides information on technical standards, archival standards, and standards for related professions.

Describing Archives: A Content Standard

Statement of Principles

The following statement of principles forms the basis for the rules in this standard. It is a recapitulation of generally accepted archival principles as derived from theoretical works and a variety of other sources. These include earlier statements about description and descriptive standards found in the reports of working groups commissioned to investigate aspects of archival description,[1] national rules for description,[2] and statements of the ICA Committee on Descriptive Standards.[3] In recognizing the disparate nature of archival holdings, the statement is also grounded in accepted professional practice in the United States.

1   Working Group on Standards for Archival Description, "Archival Description Standards: Establishing a Process for their Development and Implementation," *American Archivist* 52, no. 4 (Fall 1989) (hereinafter cited as WGSAD Report), 440–43; *Toward Descriptive Standards: Report and Recommendations of the Canadian Working Group on Archival Descriptive Standards* (Ottawa: Bureau of Canadian Archivists, 1985), 6–9, 55–59, 63–64; Wendy M. Duff and Kent M. Haworth, "Advancing Archival Description: A Model for Rationalizing North American Descriptive Standards," *Archives and Manuscripts* 25, no. 2 (1997) (hereinafter cited as the Bentley Report), 198–99, 203–4.

2   *Rules for Archival Description* (Ottawa, Bureau of Canadian Archivists, 1990), xi-xvi, rules 0.1, 0.2, 0.22, 1.0A1, 1.0A2 (hereinafter cited as RAD); Steven Hensen, comp., *Archives, Personal Papers and Manuscripts,* 2nd ed. (Chicago: Society of American Archivists, 1989), rules 0.3, 0.9, 0.10, 0.12, 1.0A (hereinafter cited as APPM).

3   ICA Statement of Principles, 8-16; ICA Committee on Descriptive Standards, *ISAD(G): General International Standard Archival Description,* 2nd ed. (Ottawa: International Council on Archives, 1999), 7–12 (hereinafter cited as *ISAD(G)*).

Holdings of archival repositories represent every possible type of material acquired from a wide variety of sources. How archives manage and describe their holdings is rooted in the nature of the materials, the context of their creation, and 200 years of archival theory. Archival descriptive practices have increasingly been applied to all the materials held by archives regardless of their provenance or method of acquisition. These principles examine the nature of archival materials and their context, and reflect how those aspects are made apparent in description.

The Nature of Archival Holdings

Archival collections are the natural result of the activities of individuals and organizations and serve as the recorded memory thereof. This distinctive relationship between records and the activities that generated them differentiates archives from other documentary resources.

Principle 1: Records in archives possess unique characteristics.

Archival material has traditionally been understood to consist of the documents organically created, accumulated, and/or used by a person or organization in the course of the conduct of affairs and preserved because of their continuing value. They most often consist of aggregations of documents and are managed as such, though archival institutions frequently hold discrete items that must also be treated consistently within the institution's descriptive system. In the course of their regular activities, individuals, archival repositories, and other institutions may also consciously acquire and assemble records that do not share a common provenance or origin but that reflect some common characteristic, for example, a particular subject, theme, or form. Such collections are part of the holdings in most institutions and must be described in a way that is consistent with the rest of the holdings. All of these materials may be described using this standard.

Principle 2: The principle of *respect des fonds* is the basis of archival arrangement and description.

The records created, accumulated, and/or maintained and used by an organization or individual must be kept together (in the sense of identified as belonging to the same aggregation) in their original order if it exists or has been maintained. They ought not be mixed or combined with the records of another individual or corporate body. This dictum is the natural and logical consequence of the organic nature of archival materials.[4] Inherent in the overarching principle of *respect des fonds* are two sub-principles—provenance and original order. The principle of provenance means that the records that were created, accumulated, and/or maintained by an organization or individual must be represented together, distinguishable from the records of any other organization or individual. The principle of original order means that the order of the records that was established by the creator should be maintained by physical and/or intellectual means whenever possible to preserve existing relationships between the documents and the evidential value inherent in their order. Together, these principles form the basis of archival arrangement and description.

In the context of this standard, the principle of provenance requires further elaboration. The statement that the records of one creator must be represented together does not mean that it is necessary (or even possible) to keep the records of one creator physically together. It does, however, mean that the provenance of the records must be clearly reflected in the description, that the description must enable retrieval by provenance, and that a descriptive system must be capable of representing together all the records of a single creator held by a single repository.

The Relationship between Arrangement and Description

If the archival functions of arrangement and description are based on the principle of *respect des fonds,* what is the relationship between arrangement and description? While the two are intimately inter-

---

4 Samuel Muller, J. A. Feith, and R. Fruin, *Manual for the Arrangement and Description of Archives,* 2nd ed., translated by Arthur Levitt, with new introductions by Peter Horsman, Eric Ketelaar, Theo Thomassen, and Marjorie Barritt, Archival Classics Series (Chicago: Society of American Archivists, 2003). "An archival collection is an organic whole."

twined, it is possible to distinguish between them in the following way. *Arrangement* is the intellectual and/or physical processes of organizing documents in accordance with accepted archival principles as well as the results of these processes. *Description* is the creation of an accurate representation of the archival material by the process of capturing, collating, analyzing, and organizing information that serves to identify archival material and to explain the context and records systems that produced it, as well as the results of these processes.

Principle 3: Arrangement involves the identification of groupings within the material.

Arrangement is the process of identifying the logical groupings of materials within the whole as they were established by the creator, of constructing a new organization when the original ordering has been lost, or of establishing an order when one never existed. The archivist then identifies further sub-groupings within each unit down to the level of granularity that is feasible or desirable, even to the individual item. This process creates hierarchical groupings of material with each step in the hierarchy described as a level. By custom, archivists have assigned names to some, but not all, levels of arrangement. The most commonly identified are collection, record group, series, file (or filing unit), and item. There may be many more levels in a large or complex body of material. The archivist must determine for practical reasons what groupings will be treated as a unit for purposes of description. These may be defined as the entire corpus of material of the creator (fonds or collection), a convenient administrative grouping (record and manuscript groups), or a reflection of administrative record-keeping systems (series and filing units).

Principle 4: Description reflects arrangement.

Archival repositories must be able to describe holdings ranging from thousands of linear feet to a single item. The amount of description and level of detail will depend on the importance of the material, management needs and resources of the repository, and access requirements of the users. That being the case, an archival description may consist of a multilevel structure that begins with a description of the whole and proceeds through increasingly more detailed descriptions of the parts, or it may consist only of a description of the whole. Within a given body of material, the repository may choose to describe some parts at a greater level of detail than others. A single item may be described in minute detail, whether or not it is part of a larger body of material.

The Nature of Archival Description

Archival holdings are varied in their nature and provenance. Archival description reflects that. If they are to be described consistently within an institutional, regional, or national descriptive system, the rules must apply to a variety of forms and media created by, and acquired from, a variety of sources.

Principle 5: Description applies to all archival materials regardless of form or medium.

It is acknowledged that archival material comes in a variety of forms and media, and rules for archival description must accommodate all forms and media (and the relationships between them). Inherent in the principle of provenance—that the records created, accumulated, and/or maintained and used by an organization or individual must be kept together—is the assumption that no records are excluded from the description because of their particular form or medium. Different media will of course require different rules to describe their particular characteristics, for example, sound recordings may require some indication of playing speed, and photographs may require some indication of polarity and color.

Principle 6: The principles of archival description apply equally to records created by corporate bodies and by individuals or families.

The documents that are the product of the functions and activities of organizations may differ in extent, arrangement, subject matter, and so on from those that result from the activities of individuals or families. While there may be valid reasons to distinguish between them in the organization of the work of a repository, the principles of archival arrangement and description should be applied equally to materials created by individuals or organizations.

Principle 7: Archival descriptions may be presented in a variety of outputs and with varying levels of detail.

The nature and origins of a body of archival materials may be summarized in their entirety in a single collective description. However, the extent and complexity of archival materials may require a more detailed description of their various components as well. The resulting technique of multilevel description is "the preparation of descriptions that are related to one another in a part-to-whole relationship and that need complete identification of both parts and the comprehensive whole in multiple descriptive records."[5] This requires some elucidation regarding the order in which such information is presented and the relationships between description(s) of the parts and the description of the whole.[6]

Principle 7.1: Levels of description correspond to the levels of arrangement.

The levels of arrangement determine the levels of description. However, because not all levels of arrangement are required or possible in all cases, it follows that not all levels of description are required. Increasingly it is understood that description is an iterative and dynamic process; that is, descriptive information is recorded, reused, and enhanced at many stages in the management of archival holdings. For example, basic information is recorded when incoming material is accessioned, well before the material is arranged. Furthermore, arrangement can change, particularly when a repository receives regular accruals of records from an ongoing organization. In that situa-

---

5 *RAD*, D-5.
6 The rules for multilevel description are found in *RAD*, rule 1.0A2 and in *ISAD(G)*, 12.

tion, the arrangement will not be complete until the organization ceases to exist. Thus, it is more appropriate to say that description reflects the current state of arrangement (whatever that may be) and can (and does) change as a result of further arrangement activities.[7]

Principle 7.2: Relationships between levels of description must be clearly indicated.

While the actual work of arrangement and description can proceed in any order that makes sense to the archivist, a descriptive system must be able to represent and maintain the relationships among the various parts of the hierarchy. Depending on where the descriptive system is entered, an end user must be able to navigate to higher and/or lower levels of description.

Principle 7.3: Information provided at each level of description must be appropriate to that level.

When a multilevel description is created, the information provided at each level of description must be relevant to the material being described. This means that it is inappropriate to provide detailed information about the contents of files in a description of a higher level. Similarly, archivists should provide administrative or biographical information appropriate to the materials being described at a given level (e.g., a series). The principle that the information provided must be relevant to its level of description also implies that it is undesirable to repeat information given at higher levels of description. To avoid needless repetition, information that is common to the component parts should be provided at the highest appropriate level.

The Creators of Archival Material

An important aspect of understanding archival materials is the description of the context in which they were created.

---

7 ISAD(G), Statement 1-3, 7.

Principle 8: The creators of archival materials, as well as the materials themselves, must be described.

If the principle of provenance is fundamental to the arrangement and description of archival materials, it follows that the provenance, or the creator(s), of archival materials must be described as well. Except in cases where the creator or collector is truly unknown, this principle means that the creator or collector of the materials must be identified and included in (or linked to) the description of the materials. Moreover, the functions and activities of the creator(s) that produced the archival materials must be described. Finally, standardized access points must be provided that indicate not just the primary creator but also the relationships between successive creators, for example, parts of a corporate body that has undergone reorganization(s). This standard includes rules for providing all of this information in a consistent way. The repository as collector does not need to be described.

Arrangement Scenarios

The following scenarios have been developed to demonstrate how one might actually carry out the defined steps for arrangement. For each hypothetical group of records, the process of making decisions about arrangement is explained in more detail. While the three sets of records are hypothetical, they mirror actual practice and address some of the common challenges faced in arrangement. These scenarios cannot cover all possible circumstances and issues that may arise in arrangement but they are intended to provide a tangible illustration of the practices and logic underpinning decisions that need to be made.

Arranging the Elsie Brown Papers

Among the challenges Susan Soporific faces as the archivist at Nodoz Historical Society is clearing up a fifty-year backlog of records donated to the society but never arranged and described. She has been offered interns by a professor at neighboring Narcoleptic University, so she decides to get out some of the smaller undescribed collections for them to process. Before putting them to work doing physical processing tasks, however, she needs to be sure they are in order so the students can do their work. Susan pulls out several sets of undescribed personal and family papers. The first group she retrieves is the Elsie Brown Papers. It consists of a cubic foot box with papers, volumes, and photographs all stacked inside in no apparent order.

Checking the accession file, she finds virtually no useful information beyond the donor agreement—which was signed in 1972 by James Brown, Jr., Elsie's son. There is fortunately a copy of the obituary for Elsie, but no other information in the accession file. From the obituary, Susan learns that Elsie was the wife of James Brown, Sr., a farmer and later a car mechanic who ran a service station in Nodoz County. She was a member of the Rebekah Lodge, the Methodist Church, and the mother of James, Eunice, and Dora Mae. Armed with that modest information, Susan looks over the records.

She spreads the materials out on her processing table and notes that they are a nice group of materials relating to the life of a woman during the Great Depression and World War II. No original order is discernible, however. She makes a quick list of the items in the box in the order she takes them out:

Elsie Brown Papers
- Recipe box with several hundred handwritten recipes (no date)
- Diary of Elsie Brown 1930–34
- Diary of Elsie Brown 1935–40
- Family photograph album 1950–55
- A large envelope filled with letters from daughter Eunice 1942
- School report cards 1910–14
- Paper clothing patterns made from newspaper (dates on the newspapers ca. 1932–35)
- School essays 1916
- Diary of Elsie Brown 1940–42
- An envelope of family photographs, 1930–35
- A large envelope filled with letters from daughter Dora

After looking over the list, Susan decides to sort them by form of material first. The groups into which she organizes the records are:

Elsie Brown Papers, 1910–1955
School records, 1910–1916
Diaries, 1930–1942
Family photographs, 1930–1955
Family letters, 1942–1944
Paper clothing patterns ca. 1932–1935
Recipes

Susan will now have an intern put the groups into archival folders and boxes and physically process the records. Because the group of records is small, she will describe them as the Elsie Brown Papers, but will not make a separate series description for each type of material she identified.

Arranging the Records of the Raisin River Railroad

John W. Garrett III, one of the members of the board of directors of the Nodoz Historical Society, is an avid fan of historic railroads. He calls the society to alert staff archivist Susan Soporific to the recent death of Hiram Banister, the former president and CEO of the Raisin River Railroad. This railroad provided local service in the region from 1900 through its demise during the 1960s. He has talked with Banister's son, William, who expressed an interest in giving the historical society the railroad materials.

William Banister invites Susan to come out and "get this stuff out of here" because he is in the process of clearing out his father's over-stuffed house. At the Banister house, William shows Susan a file cabinet and says, "Here it is. Take whatever you want, and the rest goes in the dumpster." Because of the time pressure, she does a cursory review of the records, but they look pretty good overall.

Susan packs up the boxes, being careful to put the records from each file drawer in a different box and labeling them with the information on the outside of the file drawer. Here's what she has:

Drawer 1: Financial	Drawer 4: Correspondence
Drawer 2: Advertising	Drawer 5: Miscellaneous
Drawer 3: Personnel	Drawer 6: Personal

Back at the historical society, Susan unloads the boxes, takes them into the processing area, and accessions them. It takes a few weeks for her to get back to the records to begin the arrangement process.

A cursory look at the folder titles tells her that things are pretty much in alphabetical or numerical order within their groupings. The records in the folders are generally reflected by the box titles, and she does a general check to identify the years they cover. There are two boxes that don't fit into this assessment. The box titled "Miscellaneous" appears to actually be mostly records relating to the board of directors for the railroad. The other problem is with the box labeled "Personal" because it doesn't really look like railroad records at all. A number of folders relate to Banister's schooling and family history, and several folders contain photographs.

Looking for the Original Order

Fortunately, these records were not badly disorganized in the office, and the fact that Susan was able to do the packing herself made it possible to maintain the original order as it appeared at the time. She pulls out all six boxes and takes another good look at the records. The records relating to the Raisin River Railroad seem to be in order. Most of the original file drawer labels do indeed describe the parts of the records—financial records, advertising records, personnel records, correspondence. Each original drawer has files with different colored labels and titles on each folder. These she plans to describe as series using the original titles. She has two problems: the drawer marked "Miscellaneous," and the other labeled "Personal." Once she's gone through the four well-labeled series to be sure they are in order, she'll tackle those.

With the four series, here's what she finds relating to arrangement:

Financial records: The records consist of annual budgets, income tax records, bills paid, and payroll information organized by year from 1900 to 1963.

Advertising records: The records consist of samples of all advertising done for the railroad in local newspapers and farm organization newsletters, again organized by year from 1930 to 1963.

Personnel records: These are files for each employee of the railroad, organized by name. The file is continuous from 1900 to 1963.

Correspondence: The correspondence consists of copies of letters in and out, filed together by year, and within each year by last name of correspondent.

These records are in good shape for going on with description. Susan sets those aside for later and works on the arrangement problem with the last two boxes.

The box from the file drawer marked "Miscellaneous" has six file folders with the minutes from the annual board of directors meetings, one folder for each decade. But there are also two files marked "unfiled correspondence" from 1945 and 1946, and six unlabeled file folders with about 120 photographs of the various stops along the railroad line taken over the years.

The board of directors meeting minutes can clearly be kept together as a series, since they all relate to the administrative function of the board. So that makes a fifth series of records from the Raisin River Railroad.

The unfiled correspondence does not seem to have any particular theme or reason for being separated out. However, Susan decides that it would take too much time to interfile the correspondence and that some user may someday find it important that these letters were not in the original series. So she decides to put them at the end of the "correspondence" series and to leave them with the original titles "unfiled 1945" and "unfiled 1946." The files are small enough that someone could go through them, and it also saves her from the time-consuming job of refiling correspondence.

The photographs do not seem to have been pulled from any of the existing series, so she decides to create a separate series "photographs." The folders are labeled by the stop along the railroad line, but nothing further identifies the photos aside from the year written on the back of each photograph. She'll use those folder titles and supply the inclusive years when she describes them.

Susan's final problem box is from the drawer marked "personal." The records in that box relate entirely to Hiram Banister, his school and college years, and his interest in family history. The records were just dumped into the file cabinet drawer from which she put them into a box for transporting. Literally nothing in them relates to the Raisin River Railroad, so it doesn't seem appropriate to include them in the railroad's records. Instead, she decides to arrange them as the Hiram Banister Papers. She goes through all of them first, making a list of what is there. Here is what she found:

Hiram Banister Papers:
- Report cards from Davis Road Elementary School
- Hiram's handwritten family genealogy for the Banister family done in the 1950s
- A photograph album of the 1960 Prune Peninsula Little Theater Players production of "A Raisin in the Sun"
- A photograph album of the 1959 Prune Peninsula Little Theater Players production of "Time and the River"
- College essays written by Banister on musical theater, George and Ira Gershwin, and Luigi Pirandello
- College transcripts from Prune Peninsula College
- Report cards from Raisin River High School
- A photograph album of family members including his wife Martha, his son William (labeled Billy), his father Josiah, and his mother Gertrude, his uncles Edward and Ephraim and their families

Arranging the Disorganized Papers and Putting Them in Order

Susan decides to organize the papers into three groups based on the various themes they reflect.

Here is the final arrangement pattern Susan will use for subsequent description of the records:

School and college papers: within this group she puts the records in order chronologically.

Local theater production photo albums: within this group she puts the albums in order by date of production.

Family genealogy and photograph album: she places the genealogy first, then the photograph album, since the genealogy is more comprehensive and appears to have been created before the album was assembled.

Susan now proceeds with creating finding aids for these records.

Raisin River Railroad Records, 1900–1963
   Series 1: Financial records, 1900–1963
   Series 2: Advertising records, 1930–1963
   Series 3: Personnel records, 1900–1963
   Series 4: Correspondence, 1940–1963
   Series 5: Board of Directors meeting minutes, 1900–1940
   Series 6: Photographs, 1945–1960

Hiram Banister Papers
   Series 1: School and college papers, 1928–1940
   Series 2: Prune Peninsula Little Theater Players production photograph albums, 1959–1960
   Series 3: Family genealogy and photograph album, 1950; 1960

Examples of Arrangement Patterns

Note on examples: The examples provided here reflect some of the ways archives and manuscripts are commonly arranged. The descriptions that accompany these records are all available in the on-line catalog or Web site for the institution indicated in brackets after each example. The right-hand column offers commentary about the examples.

Example 1:

Pura Belpré Papers, 1896–1985

- Personal and Biographical Information, 1919–1985
- Correspondence, 1921–1982
- Writings, 1932–1980
- Subject Files, 1896–1982
- Photographs, 1900–1980

[Centro de Estudios Puertorriquenos, Hunter College]

This arrangement reflects a common approach, with biographical information on the individual provided first, then arranged by type files. Photographs or special formats are sometimes organized as a separate series within personal papers.

EXAMPLE 2:

Eleanora Mendelssohn Papers, 1880–1949
The papers are divided into two subgroups.

Subgroup I, Personal Papers, has 5 series.
1. Personal Correspondence
2. Handwritten Notes
3. Printed Works
4. Subject Files
5. Ephemera

Subgroup II, Business Papers, has 3 series.
1. Business Papers
2. Business Correspondence
3. Bank Statements/Cancelled Checks

[Manuscripts and Archives Division, New York Public Library]

These papers are organized into two subgroups based on the individual's public and personal work.

The series are arranged by form of material.

EXAMPLE 3:

Julia Child Papers, 1920–1993
I.   Biographical
II. Correspondence
    a. Personal
    b. Cookery
    c. Fans
    d. Publishers
    e. Lawyers
    f. TV companies
III. Teaching
    a. Cooking classes
    b. TV programs
    c. Cooking demonstrations
IV. Writings
V.   Publicity

These papers are generally arranged by the various roles in Julia Child's life.

VI. Audiovisual
    a. Photographs
    b. Audiotapes
    c. Videotapes

[Schlesinger Library, Radcliffe Institute]

Audiovisual materials are often put together in papers because individuals usually keep them separate from paper files. If they had been part of paper files, however, they *would not* be pulled out to make a separate series.

EXAMPLE 4:

Bonney Family Papers, 1840–1938

Series:
I.   Samuel Bonney Papers, 1840–1864
II. Catherine V. R. Bonney Papers, 1840–1892
III. Emma C. Bonney Papers, 1880–1938

The series in this group of family papers are arranged by family member.

[Historic Cherry Hill]

EXAMPLE 5:

California Council on Criminal Justice Records, 1968–1974

Series:
Executive Director's Files, 1968–74
Law Enforcement Assistance Administration
    (LEAA) Files, 1968–73
Meeting Files, 1968–73
Subject Files, 1968–74

These records are arranged by functional series reflecting how they were maintained and used by the Council.

[California State Archives]

EXAMPLE 6:

National Association of Colored Graduate Nurses Records, 1908–1958

- Minutes
- By-Laws and Articles of Incorporation
- Correspondence -- Arranged by record
  Subseries within this series include:
  - General Correspondence
  - Correspondence on Licensure
  - Correspondence on Discrimination in Hiring
- Speeches and Testimony
- Studies and Reports
- Publications and Printed Materials

Arranged by record types and functions of the Association. The subseries is organized by the purpose of the correspondence.

[Schomburg Center for Research in Black Culture, New York Public Library]

EXAMPLE 7:

Association on American Indian Affairs Archives, 1851–1955, bulk dates 1922–1995

175 linear feet (411 archival boxes, 3 half-size boxes, ------- This group of records
11 photographic boxes, and 7 oversize boxes)

This group of records demonstrates the complexities of arranging a large body of records.

Arrangement: The Archives of the Association on American Indian Affairs are divided into five series, three of which have been divided into subseries. The contents of each series or subseries are arranged alphabetically with the exception of Series 1, Subseries 1, which is arranged hierarchically to reflect the organizational structure of the AAIA. The overall arrangement of these archives is as follows:

Series 1, Organizational Files (1922–1995)
    Subseries 1, Administration (1923–1994)
    Subseries 2, Affiliates and Offices (1922–1964)
    Subseries 3, Correspondence (1929–1995)
    Subseries 4, Finances (1933–1995)

Series 2, Subject Files (1851–1995)
    Subseries 1, General (1868–1995)
    Subseries 2, Tribal (1852–1994)
    Subseries 3, Legislation (1851–1994)
    Subseries 4, Legal Cases (1934–1991)
    Subseries 5, Programs (1927–1994)
    Subseries 6, Publications and Circulars (1924–1994)

Series 3, Personal Files (1927–1991)
    Subseries 1, Henry S. Forbes (1954–1981)
    Subseries 2, Hildegarde B. Forbes (1927–1991)
    Subseries 3, Oliver La Farge (1939–1963)
    Subseries 4, Corinna Lindon Smith (1932–1965)
    Subseries 5, Alden Stevens (1941–1971)

Series 4, Photographs (1928–1992)

Series 5, Audiovisual Material (1961–1987)

[Princeton University]

Finding Aids for Sample Records

Three sample groups of records have been provided as illustrations throughout this manual to demonstrate the major types of archival and manuscripts groups. These are "constructed" descriptions, not records that actually exist:

- Personal papers: *Charles E. Williams Papers*
  A summary bibliographic record is also provided for this record to indicate how an inventory might be reduced for use in an on-line catalog or summary guide.
- Organizational records: *Hot Coffee, Nevada, Town Clerk's Records*
- Collection: *Katherine Valdez Synchronized Swimming Collection*

INVENTORY OF THE
Charles E. Williams Papers
1909–1930

Quantity: 3 linear feet including 25 photographs

Restrictions: The Williams family retains copyright on all letters. Permission to quote from the letters must be obtained from the family.

Inventory prepared by:
Jack E. Elder
1995

Biographical history:
Charles Edward Williams was born in Coatesville, Pennsylvania, in 1900 to Willa Jackson Williams and Martin James Williams. Charles was educated in the Coatesville Public Schools, then attended Cheyney State Teachers College (now Cheyney University), receiving his B.A. in teaching in 1921. He taught in the Baltimore City schools for seven years. He then attended Howard University, receiving his J.D. in 1930. During his teaching career, Charles met and married Evelyn Jane Johnson in 1923. They had three daughters, Mary Louise (born 1925), Helen Ann (born 1926, died 1930), and Emily Jane (born 1929).

He had one older brother, George James Williams (1897–1917). George enlisted in the New York 15th Regiment of the New York Guard (the Harlem Hellfighters), which was reconstituted as the 369th U.S. Infantry during World War I. George and Charles corresponded regularly through the war until George's death as the result of a mustard gas attack.

After graduating from Howard, Charles joined two classmates, Errol Peck and James Wilson, in establishing the law firm of Peck, Williams and Wilson in Harlem. Williams focused in particular on legal services to African American musicians and artists. The firm was highly successful, eventually employing a staff of over 35 lawyers serving the Harlem community.

Williams retired in 1968 and continued to do pro bono work for Legal Aid in Harlem. He died of heart failure in 1972.

Contents Summary:
The papers consist of school report cards, essays, artwork, photographs, and reports from Williams's elementary, secondary, and college education. Also included is correspondence between Charles and his brother, George Williams, during World War I when George served in the 369th U.S. Infantry in Europe.

Series I: School and college records, 1907–1930

The papers contain records from Williams's years at Fourth Street Elementary School, Coatesville Junior and Senior High School, Cheyney State College, and Howard University.

Elementary school records include report cards for first through sixth grade. They provide letter grades for the various subjects taught. For grades three through six, the report cards also have narrative comments on Williams's performance in school.

Junior and senior high records include report cards for each grade except ninth. The report cards provide letter grades and narrative comments only for twelfth grade. Six essays written by Williams for his high school American history course are also included. They focus on the history of African American music and art in the u.s., as well as on Jim Crow policies after the Civil War. They provide insight into Williams's perspectives on the need to include African Americans in the written history of the United States.

College transcripts are included for Williams's matriculation at Cheyney State College where he majored in history education and received a B.A. Essays and reports focus on a range of topics in history from biographical essays on African American leaders to musical forms such as minstrel shows, jazz, and gospel music. Photographs of Williams, his fiancé, and his parents visiting Cheyney are included.

College transcripts relate to Williams's degree in jurisprudence at Howard University. Photographs of Williams's graduation are included.

Series II: World War I letters to and from George Williams, *1916–1917*

This series contains both copies of Charles Williams's letters to his brother George as well as letters from George to Charles relating to George's service with the 369th U.S. Infantry. The letters provide particularly important information and personal perspectives on the prejudice George experienced during training in Spartanburg, South Carolina. There is also considerable information on George's experiences when the unit fought with the 16th Division of the French Army. Letters from Charles provide stories of his experiences in school and include information on family activities. The final letter in the series is the telegram advising the Williams family of George's death.

Box list: Charles E. Williams Papers, 1907–1930

Contents	Box	Folder	Location
Series I: School and College Records			
First grade report cards	1	1	345-1-1
Second grade report cards		2	
Third grade report cards		3	
Fourth grade report cards		4	
Fifth grade report cards		5	

(continued)

Box list: Charles E. Williams Papers, 1907–1930 (continued)

Contents	Box	Folder	Location
Sixth grade report cards		6	
Seventh grade report cards		7	
Eighth grade report cards		8	
Tenth grade report cards		9	
Eleventh grade report cards		10	
Twelfth grade report cards		11	
High School history essays		12	
Cheyney State College transcripts	2	1	345-1-1
Essay on the history of minstrel shows		2	
Essay on the history of jazz		3	
Essay on the history of gospel music		4	
Photographs of Charles E. Williams at Cheyney State College		5	
Photographs of Evelyn Jane Johnson		6	
Photographs of Willa Jackson Williams and Martin James Williams at Cheyney State		7	
Howard University transcripts		8	
Graduation photographs		9	
Series II: World War I letters to and from George Williams, 1916-1917			
Letters, February 1916–March 1916	3	1	
Letters, April 1916–June 1916		2	
Letters, July 1916–September 1916		3	
Letters, October 1916–December 1916		4	
Letters, January 1917–March 1917		5	
Letters, April 1917–June 1917		6	

Summary bibliographic record for Charles E. Williams Papers

CREATOR: Williams, Charles E., 1900–1992
TITLE: Charles E. Williams Papers, 1909–1930
QUANTITY: 3 linear feet including 25 photographs

RESTRICTIONS: The Williams family retains copyright on all letters. Permission to quote from the letters must be obtained from the family.

BIOGRAPHICAL NOTE: Charles Edward Williams was born in Coatesville, Pennsylvania, in 1900 to Willa Jackson Williams and Martin James Williams. Charles was educated in the Coatesville Public Schools, then attended Cheyney State Teachers College (now Cheyney University), receiving his B.A. in teaching in 1921. He taught in the Baltimore City schools for seven years. He then attended Howard University, receiving his J.D. in 1930.

He had one older brother, George James Williams (1897–1917). George enlisted in the New York 15th Regiment of the New York Guard (the Harlem Hellfighters), which was reconstituted as the 369th U.S. Infantry during World War I. George and Charles corresponded regularly through the war until George's death as the result of a mustard gas attack.

After graduating from Howard, Charles joined two classmates, Errol Peck and James Wilson, in establishing the law firm of Peck, Williams and Wilson in Harlem and worked with Harlem musicians and artists until his retirement.

SUMMARY NOTE: The papers consist of school report cards, essays, artwork, photographs, and reports from Williams's elementary, secondary, and college education. Essays by Williams provide useful insight on his perspectives on African American music and art, and post–Civil War Jim Crow policies. Photographs of Williams, his (then) fiancée, and his parents visiting Cheyney are included.

Correspondence comprises letters between Charles and his brother, George Williams, during World War I when George served in the 369th U.S. Infantry in Europe. The letters from George provide particularly important information and personal perspectives on the prejudice George experienced during training in Spartanburg, South Carolina. There is also considerable information on George's experiences when the unit fought with the 16th Division of the French Army.

FINDING AID TO THE
HOT COFFEE, NEVADA
TOWN CLERK'S RECORDS
1891–1995

Quantity: 30 cubic feet

Organized into three series:
   Town Board Meeting Minutes, 1891–1995
   Election Records, 1920–1995
   Registration of Births and Deaths, 1891–1975

Inventory prepared by:
James Ciraolo
1997

Administrative history:

The town of Hot Coffee, Nevada, was established in 1865 by a group of former Confederate soldiers. The first mayor was John Yuma, who managed all the town's business until a population growth in the 1870s. The offices of town clerk, town board, and sheriff were established in 1872.

Two initial functions were assigned to the town clerk. The first was to maintain an official record of all the meetings of the town board. Meetings were held four times a year from 1872 until 1920. The second was to register births and deaths. This function was ended in 1975 when the state assumed all responsibility for vital records.

In 1920, the town clerk was given responsibility for maintaining the official record of town elections following the highly contested 1919 mayoral election. The clerk became responsible for overseeing the list of registered voters, the vote count, and the final recording of the election results.

Town Board Meeting Minutes, 1891–1995

10 cubic feet, including 15 5¼" floppy disks
organized chronologically

Summary: Minutes of town board meetings provide information on regular business conducted, such as discussion of budgets and financial information; reports by the mayor and the sheriff; discussion of laws; concerns and issues raised by citizens. Of particular note are minutes from meetings in 1915 addressing how to help citizens following massive damage from flooding of the Perk River. Minutes identify members as well as citizens and invited guests attending, records of votes, and rough transcripts of discussions.

Container list	Box	Folder
Minutes 1891	1	1
Minutes 1892		2
Minutes 1893		3
Minutes 1894		4
Minutes 1895		6
Minutes 1896	2	1
Etc.		

Election Records, 1920–1995

8 cubic feet (consisting of 20 bound volumes)
organized chronologically

Summary: The election records provide a list of registered voters for each year; a summary providing the total number of votes received by each candidate for each town office; and the signed oaths of office for each elected official. Records for the 1938 list of registered voters contain the names of over 100 voters who had not been in the previous year's registration list and for which fictitious addresses were supplied. Handwriting specialists from the State Police also determined that the signatures were all probably written by the same person.

Contents	Volume number
Election registration and records 1920–25	1
Election registration and records 1926–35	2
Election registration and records 1936–45	3
Election registration and records 1946–55	4
Etc.	

Registration of Births and Deaths, 1891–1975

5 cubic feet
organized chronologically by decade

Restrictions note: Access to records less that 75 years old are restricted under Nevada Laws of 1985 chapter 700. See the town clerk for information on access conditions for restricted records.

Additional physical formats available: Records were microfilmed in 1977. Users must use microfilm version.

Summary: This series consists of annual certified lists of births and a separate certified list of deaths occurring in the town of Hot Coffee.

Birth lists provide the following information from 1891–1950: name; date; mother's name; father's name; race, gender. From 1951–1975, father's name is no longer included in the list.

Death lists provide the following information: name of deceased; place of residence; place of birth (when known); cause of death; age at death; gender; marital status; certifying doctor; date of death; and individual reporting death.

Container list	Box	Folder
Contents	Box	Folder
List of births 1891–1899	1	1
List of deaths 1891–1899		2
List of births 1900–1910		3
List of deaths 1900–1910		4
List of births 1911–1920	2	1
List of deaths 1911–1920		2
Etc.		

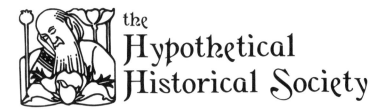

the
Hypothetical
Historical Society

Inventory for the

Katherine Valdez
Synchronized Swimming Collection
1940–1995

8 cubic feet

Prepared by: Kayla Johnson
1997

Biographical note: Katherine Valdez was born in 1940 in St. Petersburg, Florida, as the only daughter of Gustavo and Maria-Belen Valdez. She attended the Fourth Street Elementary School and graduated with a diploma from Northeast High School. In high school, she participated on many women's sports teams, including basketball, tennis, and water ballet. During the summer of her junior and senior high school years, she worked as a "mermaid" at the Weeki Wachee Springs tourist attraction. At this point in her life, she began collecting newspaper articles, photographs, and brochures about Weeki Wachee and water ballet, now known as synchronized swimming.

Valdez attended the University of Miami, earning a B.A. and M.A. in physical education. She then taught physical education at Orange Blossom High School in Gainesville, Florida, where she introduced synchronized swimming as a competitive sport for young women. She attended the University of Florida in the evenings, obtaining a PhD in physical education. Her thesis was a history of physical education for young women. Dr. Valdez taught physical education and sports history at Asuncion College from 1972 until her retirement in 1995. She was unsuccessful in her attempts to create a synchronized swimming team at Asuncion, but maintained her involvement in the sport by serving as a competition judge, eventually including the national level.

Valdez actively collected materials relating to Weeki Wachee Springs Water Park, synchronized swimming competitions at the regional, state, and national level, materials relating to Esther Williams and her movies involving swimming, and on the effort to include synchronized swimming as an Olympic sport.

Valdez retired from Asuncion College in 1995, moving back to St. Petersburg to live with her elderly parents.

Katherine Valdez Synchronized Swimming Collection, 1940–1995

8 cubic feet (400 photographs in 3 scrapbooks, 200 individual photographs, 40 videotapes, 2 movie posters, 2 cubic feet of paper records)

Records are arranged by subject:
    Weeki Wachee Springs Water Park
    Esther Williams
    Synchronized Swimming Competitions
    Olympic Status Campaign

Summary of Contents: This collection consists of photographs, records, newsclippings, movie posters and videotapes relating to the sport of synchronized swimming, originally called water ballet. Subjects addressed in the records include water ballet shows at Weeki Wachee Springs; synchronized swimming teams and competitions in Florida, the south, and nationally; Esther Williams, a water ballet swimmer who starred in Hollywood movies in the 1940s; and efforts by synchronized swimming organizations in the United States to have the sport included in the Olympics.

Three scrapbooks contain over 400 photographs of water ballet shows at Weeki Wachee Springs Water Park. The photographs show individual "mermaid" swimmers, as well as shots of the annual theme show. Show themes generally reflect popular storylines related to the ocean such as "The Little Mermaid," "Jaws," and "Cinderella of the Seas." Names of many of the performers are provided.

Several files of newsclippings, movie posters, and photographs document the career of Esther Williams. Newsclippings relate to her life and career, particularly her marriage to Fernando Lamas. Movie posters are included from *Dangerous When Wet* and *Bathing Beauty.* Photographs from the 1953 filming of *Dangerous When Wet* are also included.

40 videotapes, some rerecordings from home movie films, document synchronized swimming competitions at the collegiate level in Florida, in the Southern Zone (Alabama, Georgia, Florida, South Carolina), and at the national United States Synchronized Swimming Association meets. The tapes show team, trio, duet, and solo routines from 1965–95.

Newspaper articles, copies of petitions, positions statements, and newsletters document the efforts to have synchronized swimming made an Olympic sport.

Container List

Contents	Box	Folder
Weeki Wachee photograph scrapbook, 1956–65	1	
Weeki Wachee photograph scrapbook, 1966–80	2	
Weeki Wachee photograph scrapbook, 1981–95	3	
Newsclippings re: Esther Williams 1940–1945	4	1
Newsclippings re: Esther Williams 1946–55	4	2
Photographs re: Esther Williams 1940–50	4	3

(continued)

Container List (continued)

Contents	Box	Folder
Photographs from the set of *Dangerous When Wet* 1953	4	4
Florida collegiate competition videotapes, 1965–75	5	Tape 1: 1965 Tape 2: 1966 Tape 3: 1967 (total 10 tapes, truncated here for purposes of space)
Southern Zone competition videotapes, 1965–80	6	Tape 1: 1965 Tape 2: 1966 (total 15 tapes, truncated here for purposes of space)
USSS national competition videotapes, 1965–1975	7	Tape 1: 1965 Tape 2: 1966 (total 15 tapes, truncated here for purposes of space)
Olympic sport initiative newsclippings and newsletters	8	1
Olympic sports initiative petitions	8	2 and 3
Positions statements	8	4
Movie poster from *Bathing Beauty*	Oversize File Drawer 133	Folder 1
Movie poster from *Dangerous When Wet*	Oversize File Drawer 133	Folder 2

Examples of Bibliographic Description

Note on examples: The following examples are provided as a representative sample of descriptive practice. There is some variation among the local conventions adopted by different repositories. For example, some provide the biographical/historical note first, then the scope and content/summary note, while others do the reverse. Terminology may differ for various elements of information—for example, *scope and content note, summary, or abstract.* The examples are intended to include a range of formats that may constitute all or part of a group of records described archivally, such as paper, photographs, computer files, oral interviews, and motion pictures, but they are by no means comprehensive. They represent the type of summary descriptions generally provided in on-line catalogs. For some records, and in some repositories, finding aids will contain more detailed descriptive information. Because full finding aids for all are too extensive to include in an appendix, the reader is encouraged to look at various Web sites noted within the previous text. As with the arrangement examples, local conventions result in some differences in presentation and terminology that have been preserved here. In a few cases, subject indexing has been edited for the purposes of space, and so noted. The right-hand column offers commentary about the examples.

Personal Papers

EXAMPLE 1:

Dozier, William (1908–1991)
Papers, 1941–1977.
22 cubic ft. (49 boxes) + photographs.
Recording/Reproduction: "Batman" theme
phonograph records 45 rpm.

SUMMARY NOTE: Collection includes materials relating to Dozier's production of television programs with Greenway Productions and other television studios and companies. There are scripts, budgets, cast lists, fan mail, photographs, posters, production reports, shooting schedules, story outlines, titles and credits for "Batman" and other television programs.

Also included is correspondence with actors and others involved in Dozier's productions, with Lorenzo Semple ("Batman" writer) and Erle Stanley Gardner ("Perry Mason" writer). There are related legal documents, memos, notebooks, speeches and articles by Dozier, music notes of Nelson Riddle ("Batman" theme composer), and records of the "Batman" theme.

BIOGRAPHY/HISTORY: Dozier was a television producer who in the 1930s and early 1940s worked as a television writer and then began producing. He worked in production in several major television studios then started his own Greenway Productions in 1964. While with CBS he supervised the production of "Perry Mason," "Twilight Zone," and "Gunsmoke." His Greenway Productions worked with 20th Century Fox and produced some of the popular television programs in the 1960s including "Batman" and "Green Hornet."

Other Author(s):

West, Adam.

Serling, Rod, 1924–.

Selznick, David O., 1902–1965.

Lee, Bruce, 1940–1973.

Bridges, Lloyd.

Semple, Lorenzo.

Gardner, Erle Stanley, 1889–1970.

> These individuals are listed as "other authors" because they wrote some letter or item in the records.

Other Titles:

Perry Mason (Television program)

Loner (Television program)

Heaven Help Us (Television program)

Tammy Grimes Show (Television program)

You're Only Young Twice (Television program)

Dick Tracy (Television program)

Batman (Theme)

Subjects:

Riddle, Nelson.

Ward, Burt.

Greenway Productions.

Television Production and
    Direction—United States.

Television scripts.

Television programs—United States.

Popular culture.

Scripts. [aat]. -- This is a form of mate-

Television producers and directors. [lcsh]. ------- rial term drawn from the *Art and Architecture Thesaurus*.

> These individuals are listed as subjects because there is information *about* them in the records, but they did not themselves create any of the information in the records.

Notes: Finding aid available in repository.

[American Heritage Center, University of Wyoming]

> This is an occupation term drawn from the *Library of Congress Subject Headings*.

EXAMPLE 2:

Durr, Virginia Foster
Papers, 1904–1991.
13 cubic ft. (4 archives boxes, 1 oversized folder.)

GENERAL NOTE: Some Hugo L. Black correspondence and all Lyndon B. and Lady Bird Johnson correspondence photocopied.

This general note alerts the user to the fact that some correspondence is not the original copy.

BIOGRAPHICAL NOTE: Durr was born on 1903 Aug. 5 to the Presbyterian minister Sterling J. and Anne Patterson Foster in Birmingham, Jefferson Co., Alabama. She attended public schools in Birmingham, the National Cathedral School in Washington, D.C., then Wellesley College. On 1926 Apr. 5 she married Clifford J. Durr. In the early 1930s she was active in getting the Birmingham Junior League to begin a free milk project and free music concerts.

In 1933 the Durrs moved to Washington, D.C., where Virginia became active in the women's division of the Democratic National Committee. She was also active in the Southern Conference for Human Welfare from 1938 forward, and at its founding in 1939 became Vice-Chair of the Committee to Abolish the Poll Tax. After World War II she became interested in the peace movement, especially in opposing the U.S. continuing involvement in the Korean War. Her primary concern in the 1950s and 1960s, however, remained civil rights, especially voting rights for blacks and poor whites in the South. She actively worked in that effort.

She and her husband had five children. One child, Cliff, Jr., was born in 1935, but died in 1938. Their other children, in order of birth, were Anne Patterson, who married Walter A. Lyon; Lucy Judkins, who married F. Sheldon Hackney; Virginia

Foster, who married Frank R. Parker III; and Lulah Johnston, who married Richard V. Colan.

SUMMARY NOTE: These papers contain correspondence, letters, clippings, photographs, awards, certificates, ephemera, and printed materials. The primary topics discussed are her family and friends, civil rights and voting in the South, and politics in the U.S. and in Alabama. Correspondence and letters constitute one-half of the collection, and clippings one-fourth. Of particular interest is the correspondence with the Harkness Fellows, who were European students studying in the U.S., as well as the correspondence with Hugo L. Black, and his second wife, Elizabeth, and with Lyndon and Lady Bird Johnson.

> This note points out research strengths to the user.

Other prominent correspondents included: Julian Bond, Angus Cameron, William Sloan Coffin, John Doar, James Dombrowski, William O. Douglas, James E. Folsom, Abe Fortas, John Hope Franklin, Helen Fuller, Katherine Graham, Grover Cleveland Hall Sr., Estes Kefauver, Herbert H. Lehman, David E. Lilienthal, Carey McWilliams, Arthur Miller, Drew Pearson, Walker Percy, Claude Pepper, Albert Raines, Richard T. Rives, Pete Seeger, Eleanor Roosevelt, John Sparkman, Harlan F. Stone, Studs Terkel, and William Allen White.

> The names of these individuals appear in the indexing; many repositories have chosen to list the names in the scope note so the user will know why the record has been retrieved in an on-line catalog search.

Unrestricted.

Series descriptions, container listing, and index available in repository.

Related materials in Schlesinger Library, Radcliffe College: Virginia F. Durr Papers; and in Lyndon B. Johnson Presidential Library.

> This note provides the user with information on other records related by provenance to these records, but held by a different repository.

OTHER AUTHORS:
Bond, Julian, 1940–.
Brecher, Edward M.
Cameron, Angus.
Coffin, William Sloan, 1924–.
Colan, Lulah Johnston Durr, 1942–.
Dabbs, Edith.
Doar, John.
Dombrowski, James, 1897–1983.
Douglas, William O. (William Orville), 1898–.
(etc.)

SUBJECTS: *(subject indexing edited for purposes of space)*
Durr, Clifford J. (Clifford Judkins), 1899–1975.
Eastland, James O. (James Oliver), b.1904.
Rice family.
Wallace, George C. (George Corley), 1919–.
Junior League (Birmingham, Ala.).
Southern Conference on Human Welfare.
United States. Federal Communications Commission.
United States. Reconstruction Finance Corporation.
United States. Supreme Court.
Civil Rights—Alabama.
Civil Rights—United States.
Congresses and conventions —Alabama— Birmingham.
Congresses and conventions —USSR—Moscow.
Dating (Social customs).
Education—Alabama.
Family—Alabama.
Korean War, 1950–1953—Protest movements.
Poll-tax —Alabama.
Presidents—United States—Election.
Race relations.

Racism—Alabama.
Suffrage—Alabama.
Suffrage—Southern states.
Trade-unions—United States.
Alabama—Economic conditions.
Alabama—History.
Alabama—Politics and government.
Europe—Description and travel.
United States—History—20th century.
United States—Politics and government—
   20th century.
Union of Soviet Socialist Republics—
   Description and travel.
Clippings.
Correspondence.
Letterheads.
Letters.

Geographic index terms such as these can be helpful to users; such access is often overlooked in archival indexing, but in some repositories is a frequent route by which users seek information.

[Alabama Dept. of Archives and History]

EXAMPLE 3:

Marshall, Jonathan, 1924–
Papers 1972–1975 [manuscript].
4 ft.

NOTE: Composed of correspondence, newsclippings, printed matter, computer printouts and notebooks concerning Marshall's 1974 campaign for the United States Senate. Subject files contain materials pertaining to subjects identified by Mr. Marshall or his staff.

The item in brackets is a "general material designator." Providing this is particularly useful when archives and manuscripts are included in a general library catalog with books and other published materials. It clarifies for students that the materials are not the traditional published items they commonly use in the library.

Arranged alphabetically by subject and chronologically within file folders. Miscellaneous materials follow, comprised of notebooks, computer printouts, information packets, newsclippings and audiovisual materials.

This arrangement statement gives a user a sense of how hard or easy it may be to locate information on the research topic.

BIOGRAPHICAL NOTE: Publisher and editor of the *Scottsdale Daily Progress*. Born in New York City in 1924, Jonathan Marshall received his B.A. in economics and political science from the University of Colorado. In 1953 he purchased the *Arts Digest,* changed its title to *Arts,* and managed the publication for five years. He reentered school in 1958 in order to complete his M.A. in journalism. In 1963, Marshall began his career as editor and publisher of the *Scottsdale Daily Progress.* Elected president of the Arizona Newspaper Association in 1972, he has also served as chair of the ANA Legislative and Freedom of Information Committees. Marshall has served on the boards of several civic groups as well as being an active member of the Scottsdale Chamber of Commerce.

Again, note that the emphasis in the biographical note pertains only to information about the individual that relates to the records, not his entire life.

Unpublished register available.

SUBJECTS:
  Babbitt, Bruce E.
  Goldwater, Barry M. (Barry Morris), 1909–.
  Beaty, Orren.
  Rothstein, Joseph M.
  Marshall, Maxine.
  Democratic National Committee (U.S.).
  Democratic Party (Ariz.).
  Navajo Tribal Council.
  Gray Panthers.
  Common Cause (U.S.).
  Rowan Group.

United States. Congress—Elections, 1974.
Scottsdale Daily Progress.
Publishers and publishing—Arizona—
     Scottsdale—Archives.
Journalists—Arizona—Scottsdale—Archives.
Watergate Affair, 1972–1974.
Political campaigns—Arizona.

[Arizona State University]

EXAMPLE 4:

Fitzhugh, Lucy Stuart
Scrapbook, 1861–1908.   -- This description
                                                          provides an example
1 v.   of a manuscript group
                                                          consisting of only
HISTORICAL NOTE: School teacher of Lexington,   one item.
Kentucky.

                                                          This note provides
                                                          minimal information,
SUMMARY NOTE: Included are the charter and by-   and may be all that
laws of the Lexington Chapter of the United   is known about the
Daughters of the Confederacy; papers of her father,   individual.
Captain Robert Hunter Fitzhugh, CSA, about his
Civil War service and work as an engineer after the
war; Fitzhugh family information; and newspaper
clippings about the Confederacy.

SUBJECTS:
     Confederate States of America. Army—
          History—Sources.
     Fitzhugh family.
     Fitzhugh, Robert Hunter, b. 1836.
     Kentucky—History—Civil War,
          1861–1865—Societies, etc.
     United Daughters of the Confederacy.
          Lexington Chapter (Lexington, Ky.).

[Filson Club Historical Society Manuscript Dept.]

EXAMPLE 5:

William and Elizabeth Peters

Fonds 1830–1831, copied [19--], microfilmed 1961. ┈┈ This statement pro-
1 cm of textual records.   vides a very clear
                      understanding of
                      when the diaries were
SCOPE AND CONTENT: Fonds consists of mimeo-   written, when copied
graph copies of the two diaries of husband and   (approximate) and
wife, William and Elizabeth Peters, written during when microfilmed.
their voyage from England to Canada in 1830.
William's diary provides an account of fishing ves-
sels off the Newfoundland coast and an encounter
with a Spanish Man-of-War. Elizabeth's diary
describes conditions on board the ship. Fonds also
includes a letter, dated 1831, from William to
Richard Peters in England.

BIOGRAPHICAL SKETCH: William and Elizabeth
Peters were English immigrants who came to
Canada in 1830 and eventually settled in Hope,
Durham County, where William became a farmer
and itinerant preacher.

TERMS FOR USE AND REPRODUCTION: Copyright ┈ This statement is an
held by creator. These materials cannot be pub- example of adminis-
lished without permission of the copyright holder. trative information
                      giving the user infor-
                      mation on restrictions
Availability of other formats: Fonds is also avail- relating to use of the
able in microfilm version.   documents.

[Archives of Ontario]

Example 6:

Creator: Guyton de Morveau, Louis Bernard, baron, 1737–1816.
Title: Letters to Guyton de Morveau, 13 and 17 March 1792.
Quantity: 2 items.

Morveau is identified as the creator because he received, used, and kept the letters as part of his professional work. The individuals who wrote the actual letters are identified in the index terms as "other authors."

Biographical note: French chemist, remembered chiefly for reforming chemical nomenclature.

The biographical note here only addresses the part of his life relating to these letters.

Summary: Two letters concerning the soap trade in Marseille, one signed "Bernard," the other signed by the mayor and other municipal officials of Marseille. Guyton de Morveau apparently had been asked to adjudicate claims of impurities in the soap.

The description provides some context on why the letters may have been written.

Related item: Mémoire que les négocians soussignés, qui font exploiter des fabriques de savon à Marseille, présentent au Roi & à la nation française, 1789.

Subjects:
    Soap trade—France—Marseille.
    Marseille (France)—History—18th century.

Other authors: Bernard.

Organizational Records

EXAMPLE 7:

CREATOR: Tin Can Tourists of the World.
TITLE, DATES: Records 1920–1982.
AMOUNT: 2.25 cubic ft.
ORGANIZATION/ARRANGEMENT: By record type.

BIOGRAPHICAL/HISTORICAL: The Tin Can Tourists of the World (T.C.T.) was an organization of camping and "trailering" enthusiasts founded at a Tampa, Florida campground in 1919. The goals of the group were to provide its members with safe and clean camping areas, wholesome entertainment, and high moral values.

The origin of the term "tin can" in the name is not clear. One school of thought contends that it refers to the campers' reliance upon canned foods. Another school asserts that it refers to the small Ford automobile of the era, the Model T or "Tin Lizzie," which was the car of the middle class from which the majority of T.C.T. members came. The original recognition emblem of the T.C.T. was a tin can soldered to the radiator cap of a member's car.

The group usually held at least two meetings a year. A winter meeting was held at a campground in Florida and a summer meeting was held at a campground in Michigan. The Florida meetings were held in various places, including Tampa, Sarasota, Ocala, and Eustis. These meetings provided the opportunity for transacting official club business and taking part in the numerous social activities offered. For many years these club gatherings provided places of exhibition to the manufacturers of trailers, mobile homes, and camping gear. This aspect of the gatherings continued until after

This description summarized all the existing records of this organization. As the amount is small, they are described at the record group level.

The organizational history provides a statement of this group's function.

World War II when manufacturers' trade shows took the place of exhibiting at T.C.T. meetings.

The Tin Can Tourists of the World was at one time the largest organization of its kind but is now defunct.

SUMMARY: This collection contains the records of the Tin Can Tourists of the World (T.C.T.) from 1920 to 1982. The records consist of scrapbooks, photographs, convention programs, necrology (memorial) service programs, official records (constitution, by-laws, minutes), correspondence, and an early membership list. The scrapbooks contain the bulk of the information available. It documents the functions of the T.C.T., the various camp sites where meetings were held, the evolution of the trailers used and the automobiles that towed them, and the activities and amusements enjoyed by the members.

The materials of an official nature are limited. The minutes cover only a few dates of the officers' meetings. The correspondence is similarly meager in scope. However, there is a set of convention and necrology programs for the period of 1940 to 1975 that contain the names of the officers and the recently deceased members for the years covered.

FINDING AIDS: Folder listing available.

OWNERSHIP/CUSTODIAL HISTORY: These materials had been included in a donation to the Museum of Florida History by Ray and Mary Levett on July 3, 1986.

This summary begins by identifying the types of records commonly found.

The summary note provides information on limitations of the contents to assist potential users.

This description provides administrative information on who donated records. Some repositories do not include this information in their descriptions to protect the privacy of donors, and to discourage others from contacting them.

SUBJECT ACCESS FIELDS:
  Outdoor recreation—Florida.
  Trailer camps.
  Tourist trade—Florida.
  Travel trailers—Societies, etc.
  Scrapbooks. aat.
  Tampa (Fla.).
  Ocala (Fla.).
  Sarasota (Fla.).
  Eustis (Fla.).
  Hillsborough County (Fla.).
  Lake County (Fla.).
  Marion County (Fla.).
  Sarasota County (Fla.).

[Florida State Archives]

EXAMPLE 8:

Brown's Studio
Photographs, 1942–1963.
35 images.

BACKGROUND: Under the system of racial segregation that existed in much of the American South from the late 19th century until the 1960s and 1970s, many public accommodations such as buses, elevators and restaurants were segregated by law. Many other areas of life were segregated by custom, and many businesses catered to one race or the other. In the African American community, many banks, insurance companies, funeral parlors, and photo studios served an exclusively African American clientele. One such photo studio, Brown's, made the photographs in this collection. Located on 17th Street North in Birmingham,

This provides a good example of when photographs are described using archival principles. Although limited images have survived, they were all created by the Brown's Studio in the course of doing their business. This gives the group of photographs a relationship and context that is important information for the user.

Alabama (in part of the downtown black business district of the time), the studio was operated by Leon W. Brown from about 1938 until about 1968.

This organizational history note provides the context indicating why this particular photographic studio has historical significance.

SCOPE AND CONTENT: This collection contains 36 images, a tiny fraction of the total number of images that a professional photographer like Leon Brown would have created. The photographs in this collection are all group portraits showing the Birmingham Motion Picture Machine Operator's Union, Fairfield Industrial High School students, Praco High School students, Madam C. J. Walker Beauty College students, and graduating classes from Parker High School and Ullman High School. These schools were all reserved for African Americans.

RELATED COLLECTIONS:
BIRMINGFIND PROJECT Photographs
COMMON BONDS PROJECT Photographs

SUBJECT AREAS:
    African Americans—Alabama—Birmingham.
    African Americans—Education—Alabama—
        Birmingham.
    Fairfield Industrial High School (Fairfield, Ala.).
    Parker High School (Birmingham, Ala.).
    Photographers.
    Praco High School (Birmingham, Ala.).
    Ullman High School (Birmingham, Ala.).

SOURCE: Vester Brown

RESTRICTIONS: Standard preservation and copy right restrictions.

GUIDE PREPARED BY: Alan Couch
    (September 2002)

Some archival organizations provide the name of the individual preparing the description in their finding aid.

[Birmingham Public Library]

EXAMPLE 9:

Ulster County (N.Y.) Clerk's Office.
Marriage books, (c. 1908–1935).
QUANTITY: 4 volumes, 2.20 cubic feet.
ARRANGEMENT: Chronological.
MEDIUM: Handwritten under printed headings.

Marriage books are marriage docket books that reveal all the pertinent information concerning marriages in Ulster County including full name, color, place of residence, age, occupation, place of birth, name of father, father's birthplace, maiden name of mother, mother's birthplace, and the number of marriages and divorces for both the groom and the bride. Also included are date of license, date of marriage, place of marriage, official presiding and the official's professional status. Each book contains 5,000 records.

SEE: Marriage Index database.
SEE: Marriage Certificates (Licenses).

[Ulster County Clerk's Office Archives]

This provides an example of local government records description. It describes a series created by the Ulster County Clerk's Office. Because the records of that office are so extensive, they are described at the series level rather than at the record group level.

This description lists the standardized information provided in the Marriage Books.

This description points users to a related access tool (the Marriage Index database) and to a related series (Marriage Certificates).

EXAMPLE 10:

Atlanta Hillel.
Atlanta Hillel records, 1963—1988.
1.25 linear ft. (in 2 boxes)

This group of records is small and has been described at the record group level.

HISTORICAL NOTE: Atlanta Hillel, an organization for Jewish College students in Atlanta, Georgia, includes students from Emory University, Georgia State University, Georgia Institute of Technology, and Oglethorpe University.

SUMMARY NOTE: The collection consists of records of Atlanta Hillel from 1963–1988. The files include membership applications, correspondence, subject files, public relations materials, budget reports, and information on the programs at Georgia Tech, Oglethorpe University, and Emory University.

Files also include papers of the Reformed Jewish Students Committee (ca. 1982–1984) and pledge cards from the Jewish dental fraternity, Alpha Omega (ca. 1963–1977).

Finding aid available in repository.
Transfer, 1990. --

Some archival institutions include administrative information in their finding aids such as this on the date of transfer.

SUBJECTS:
  Alpha Omega (Fraternity).
  Emory University.
  Georgia Institute of Technology.
  Oglethorpe University (Atlanta, Ga.).
  Reformed Jewish Students Committee of Emory.
  Jewish college students—Georgia.
  Jews—Georgia—Social life and customs.
  Jews—Georgia—Societies, etc.
  Universities and colleges—Georgia—Societies, etc.
  Atlanta (Ga.).

[Emory University]

EXAMPLE 11:

Claflin College (Orangeburg, S.C.) Board of Trustees

Board of Trustees minutes, [ca. 1870]–1987 ················ The inclusive dates
(bulk 1870–1960).
3 v.

NOTES: Part of the Cooperative HBCU Archival
Survey Project (CHASP) to survey the archival collections housed in the Historically Black Colleges
and Universities (HBCUs).

HISTORICAL NOTE: Founded as Claflin University
on Dec. 18, 1869 in Orangeburg, S.C. by the Freed-
men's Aid Society of the Methodist Episcopal
Church; est. largely through the generosity of
Boston philanthropist, the Hon. Lee Claflin and
his son, Massachusetts Governor William Claflin;
occupies the former site of the Orangeburg
Female Seminary; in 1871 merged with Baker
Biblical Institute, founded in 1866 in Charleston,
S.C., but later moved to Orangeburg, and with a
training school in Camden, S.C.; from 1872 to 1896
Claflin was affiliated with the South Carolina
College of Agriculture and Mechanics Institute
For Colored Students (later to become South
Carolina State University) which began as a
department of Claflin University, organized by the
State of South Carolina to educate its Negro citi-
zens in order to receive federal funds for educa-
tion; name changed to Claflin College in 1979 and
back to Claflin University in 1999.

SUMMARY: Minutes are contained in bound volumes 1870–1915, 1916–1960, and 1984–1987. Topics
discussed include curriculum development, elimi-

The inclusive dates
begin with an approxi-
mate date, and also
provide bulk dates to
aid the user.

This note provides the
user with administra-
tive information on
how this description
was developed.

This historical note
provides a good
example of the com-
plex background of
some organizations,
with mergers, name
changes and affila-
tions that are impor-
tant to know when
using the records.

This description
points out major
topics found in the
minutes.

nation of primary and secondary grades, building construction, funding, affiliation with Methodist Church, and administrative and faculty appointments.

Restricted access. By appointment only. ---------------- This note forewarns a user who finds this record in an on-line catalog that contact with the library is needed to see the records; it is a physical access restriction, not related to copyright.

Finding aid is not available. ------------------

Cite as: Board of Trustees minutes, Claflin University Archives, Claflin University.

SUBJECTS:

This note lets the user know there is no further descriptive information on these records.

    Minutes—South Carolina—Orangeburg. aat.
    Claflin University —Administration.
    Claflin College (Orangeburg, S.C.)—
        Administration.
    Claflin University—Faculty.
    Claflin College (Orangeburg, S.C.)—Faculty.
    Methodist Church (U.S.).
    United Methodist Church (U.S.).
    African American Universities and Colleges—
        South Carolina—Orangeburg.
    African American college administrators—
        Selection and appointment—
            South Carolina— Orangeburg.
    African American college teachers—Selection
        and appointment—South Carolina—
        Orangeburg.
    College administrators—Selection and
        appointment—South Carolina—
        Orangeburg.
    College teachers—Selection and appointment—
        South Carolina—Orangeburg.
    Methodist Universities and Colleges—
        South Carolina—Orangeburg.
    Private Universities and Colleges—
        South Carolina—Orangeburg.

African Americans—Education (Higher)—
South Carolina—Orangeburg.
College buildings—South Carolina—
Orangeburg.
College trustees—South Carolina—
Orangeburg.
Curriculum planning—South Carolina—
Orangeburg.

OTHER AUTHORS: Claflin University. Board of
Trustees.

LOCATION: Claflin College, Claflin College
Archives, H. V. Manning Library
(Orangeburg, s.c.).

EXAMPLE 12:

Latvian National Federation in Canada Fonds
1947–1988.
7.2cm of textual records
18 audiocassettes .... This information lets
users know the types
of materials in the
fonds.

SCOPE AND CONTENT: Fonds consists of the
records created and received by the Latvian
National Federation in Canada. Fonds includes
the organization's constitution, resolutions, by-
laws, meetings, minutes, annual reports, correspondence, membership files, and bulletins. Also
included are records from the following bureaux:
Education, Culture, Political Information, Youth,
Immigration/Relief, and Economics. Fonds also
contains some administrative records of the
Latvian Relief Association.

In addition, fonds contains audiocassettes of oral histories.

Administrative history: The Latvian National Federation in Canada (lnak) was established in Toronto, Ontario in 1950 to encourage Latvian immigration to Canada and to assist Latvian immigrants, as well as to support the cause of Latvian independence from the Soviet Union.

This note points out the organization's function.

Restrictions on access: Records are closed for fifteen years after the date of their creation unless otherwise stated.

This note forewarns users that they may not be able to look at all records in the fonds.

Notes: All records are in Latvian unless otherwise noted.

Finding aid: An inventory is available for this fonds.

Example 13:

New York (State). Education Dept. Information Center on Education.
Basic Educational Data Systems personnel master file, 1968–1981 [computer file].
14 magnetic tape reels

The information in brackets is a general material designator, forewarning users that these records are not in a paper format.

Arrangement: Chronological by year, then alphabetical by county.

Abstract: The Basic Educational Data System (beds) Personnel Master File contains detailed data on the demographic and professional characteristics of public school professional staff and data on their teaching and non-teaching assignments.
     Each record consists of two sections: a header section identifying the professional's name, sex,

Although the tapes are extensive, the information they contain is quite standardized and can be listed succinctly.

marital status, age, educational level, and professional experience; and a main section with assignment data such as the assignment code, assignment name, grade level of students, ability levels of students, and the professional's assignment certification status.

The Archives will also provide copying of the data files on magnetic tape or floppy disk and copying of any support documentation. A user's guide is available from the State Archives.

TAPE CHARACTERISTICS: The Personnel Master File contains 14 rectangular flat files stored in Standard label EBCDIC. The files contain numeric and character data. The files are stored on 14 reels of tape at 6250 bpi. The data can be manipulated using a common statistical package. Tape copies are in standard label EBCDIC format. Floppy disk copies are in ASCII format.

ACCESS RESTRICTION: Restricted: Some personal data on teachers is restricted.

FINDING AIDS: User's guide.

SUBJECTS:
School employees—New York (State).
Students—New York (State).
Elementary school teaching—New York (State).
High school teaching—New York (State).

FORM/GENRE TERMS: Magnetic tapes. aat.
FORM/GENRE TERMS: Machine-readable records. aat.

FUNCTION TERMS: Teaching. aat.

CORPORATE AUTHOR: University of the State of New York.

This provides important information for users on how to obtain the information in this series.

Electronic records often require support information such as this guide for users.

Additional physical descriptive information is often needed for electronic records.

Collections

EXAMPLE 14:

Hayter, Earl W.
Collection, 1866–1958.
1.3 cubic ft. (2 boxes)

These are inclusive dates indicating the period covered by the collection.

COLLECTION SUMMARY NOTE: Collection contains papers (1878–1903) of Isaac Ellwood, inventor and manufacturer of barbed wire, especially those documents pertaining to contracts to provide barbed wire fencing for various railroad rights of way, and to some of Ellwood's mining interests in Idaho and Mexico (Honest John Mining & Milling Co. and Creston-Colorada Co.) Also included are papers (1866–1900) of Charles W. Marsh, inventor and manufacturer of harvesters; advertising and other documents of various wire and agricultural machinery manufacturers such as Jacob Haish, R. H. Pooler and others (1878–ca. 1927); short histories of barbed wire development and of De Kalb County, Illinois (1923–1958); and 3 photo albums of specimens of early barbed wire (1929).

This note summarizes the various papers and items collected by Hayter as part of his research.

BIBLIOGRAPHIC NOTE: Earl W. Hayter was a professor at the Northern Illinois State Teachers College (later Northern Illinois University) in De Kalb, Illinois. He studied and wrote about the history of barbed wire fencing, which was first extensively manufactured in the De Kalb area, and about farming and farm machinery. Hayter acquired many documents relating to early inventors and manufacturers of barbed wire and farm machinery.

This note explains why Hayter collected this type of material.

Finding aid available in repository.

SUBJECTS:

Ellwood, Isaac L., 1833–1910.

Haish, Jacob, 1826–1926.

Pooler, R. H.

Marsh, Charles W., 1834–.

Creston-Colorada Company.

Honest John Mining and Milling Company.

American Steel & Wire Co.

Ellwood Manufacturing.

Kankakee and Seneca Railroad.

St. Louis and Southwestern Railroad
Company.

Texas Midland Railroad.

Washburn and Moen Manufacturing
Company.

Barbed wire.

Harvesting machinery.

Agricultural machinery.

De Kalb County (Ill.)

[American Heritage Center, University of Wyoming]

EXAMPLE 15:

Glengarry County History Collection

1811–1934.

15 cm of textual records.

SCOPE AND CONTENT: The Glengarry County collection is an artificial creation of the Archives of Ontario and consists of originals and copies of records relating to the history of Glengarry County. Collection contains diaries, correspondence and legal documents of various Glengarry County families. Families represented include: Kippen, McDiarmid, McEwen, Cameron, McLeod,

This is typical of the regional collections created in many historical societies and archives. The organization itself has amassed this group of records to document the county.

and MacMillan. The collection also includes a rural mail directory for Stormont and Glengarry Counties, 1927, as well as historical notes on Glengarry County by Angus "Bahn" McDonnell.

[Archives of Ontario]

EXAMPLE 16:

CREATOR: Ford, Allyn Kellogg, 1878–1964, collector.

The specific role "collector" is provided here to immediately clarify Ford's role to users.

TITLE: Allyn Kellogg Ford collection of historical manuscripts, 1472–1970.

DESCRIPTION: 5 microfilm reels.

SUMMARY: More than 1500 letters, cards, and documents of noted politicians, authors, colonial and Revolutionary War figures, soldiers, explorers, scientists, educators, business leaders, clergymen, and others prominent in cultural and public affairs, collected by Minneapolis businessman Allyn K. Ford. They span several continents, although most are from United States personalities, and the majority are of historical as well as autograph value. Among them are letters or documents from many noted Revolutionary War figures, including a number to General George Weedon, George Washington's aide-de-camp during the 1781 Yorktown campaign; from most U.S. Presidents, some of their wives, and a variety of letters to Grover Cleveland's sister Rose; from many classic American and British authors; and from assorted European political figures and heads of state. There is discussion of various aspects of science and exploration; long, detailed letters on the Mexican War; letters about life and politics in

This is typical of the work of an historical manuscript "collector" who amassed records of famous individuals or eras.

several Asian countries; legal documents of colonial America and early modern Europe; and a 16th century illuminated manuscript.

ORIGINAL-NOTE: Originals are in the Minnesota Historical Society.

This description is for the microfilmed version of this collection.

INDEXING-NOTE: An item list, a file of calendar sheets, and indexes by subject, type of author, and (selectively) place written from are available in the repository; filed under M316.

This note provides users with information on more detailed indexing tools available.

[Minnesota Historical Society]

EXAMPLE 17:

Agency History Record with examples of associated series descriptions

Missouri. Commission on Human Rights.

TITLE: Agency history record, 1957–present.

NOTES: The Missouri Commission on Human Rights enforces Missouri's anti-discrimination statutes, and cooperates with other organizations to discourage discrimination and encourage fair treatment for all persons. The Commission operates alongside the Department of Labor and Industrial Relations. 1957–present.

FUNCTION, MISSION AND MANDATE: The Missouri Commission on Human Rights enforces Missouri's anti-discrimination statutes which forbid discrimination in housing, employment, and public accommodations on the basis of race, color, religion, national origin, ancestry, sex, handicap, age (in employment only) or familial status (in housing only). The functions of the commission are to cooperate with other organizations to discourage discrimination, to conduct research projects, to make studies and public reports on discrimination in Missouri, to receive and investigate complaints of discrimination, to recommend ways of eliminating injustice, to hold public hearings, and to encourage fair treatment for all persons. The commission has the power to order affirmative relief to eliminate discrimination.

ORGANIZATIONAL HISTORY: The commission was created by the 69th General Assembly in 1957 and was made a permanent agency in 1959. The commission consists of 11 members with at least one member from each of the state's nine congressional districts. Commissioners are nominated for six-year terms by the director of the Department of Labor and Industrial Relations. Commissioners are appointed by the governor and confirmed by the Senate. They serve without compensation.

The records of this agency are described separately and are linked to this agency history.

SUBJECTS:
Discrimination—Missouri.
Age discrimination in employment—Missouri.
Discrimination in education—Missouri.
Discrimination in employment.
Discrimination in housing—Missouri.
Discrimination in public accommodations —
    Missouri.
Race discrimination.
Sex discrimination.

Human rights — Missouri.
State government records. aat.
Missouri Department of Labor and Industrial
Relations.

Missouri. Commission on Human Rights.

TITLE: Tape recordings of commission meetings,
1974–1977.

DESCRIPTION: 2.5 cubic ft. 5 hollinger boxes legal size.

RESTRICTION NOTES: This record series is restricted.
Any use must be approved by the executive director of
the Missouri Commission on Human Rights.

NOTES: Cassette tape recordings of regular and executive
meetings of the commission. Also contains recordings of
appeals or termination.

Descriptive inventory. Unpublished guide available in
repository. Photocopy may be purchased from repository (1 page).

SUBJECTS:
Missouri Commission on Human Rights.
Discrimination—Missouri.
Age discrimination in employment—Missouri.
Discrimination in education—Missouri.
Discrimination in employment—Missouri.
Discrimination in housing—Missouri.
Discrimination in public accommodations—
Missouri.
Race discrimination—Missouri.
Sex discrimination—Missouri.
Sex discrimination—Missouri.
Human rights—Missouri.

State government records. aat.
Minutes. aat.

Missouri. Commission on Human Rights.

TITLE: Scrapbooks and photographs, 1958–1975.

DESCRIPTION: 6 cubic ft., 15 small flat storage boxes.

NOTES: Scrapbook for 1973 is missing.
Series contains newspaper clippings on the commission and other human rights issues. One volume of photographs is also included, consisting of members and activities.

Descriptive inventory. Unpublished guide available in repository. Photocopy may be purchased from repository (1 page).

SUBJECTS:
Missouri Commission on Human Rights.
Human Rights—Missouri.
Discrimination—Missouri.
State government records. aat.
Photographs. aat.
Scrapbooks. aat.

Index

Boldface indicates figures and tables.

About the Author

Kathleen Roe is Chief of Archival Services at the New York State Archives where she manages the operation of the State Archives facility, including its reference, description, and access programs. She also manages programs providing training and advisory services to local government archives and historical records programs statewide, and coordinates efforts to document New York's underrepresented communities. She received a BA and MA in history from Michigan State University, and an MLS in archival administration from Wayne State University. Her record of service in the archival profession includes: president of the Council of State Historical Records Coordinators and chair for the National Forum on Archival Continuing Education, chair of several committees of the Society of American Archivists, including the Committee on Archival Information Exchange and the Appointments Committee, as well as serving on the SAA Task Force on Diversity. She was elected as a Fellow of the Society of American Archivists and has been a member of several national and international archival practices research projects. She has published and taught workshops in the areas of archival descriptive practices, archival continuing education, and the use of historical records with students.